By the same author

Poetry
Sheltering Places
The Lundys Letter
Sunday School
Heart of Hearts

Essays
Stray Dogs and Dark Horses:
Selected Shorter Prose

AGAINST PIETY

Essays in Irish Poetry

GERALD DAWE

Gerald Dawe

LAGAN PRESS
BELFAST
1995

Published by
Lagan Press
PO Box 110 BT12 4AB, Belfast

The publishers wish to acknowledge the financial assistance of the Arts Council of Northern Ireland in the production of this book.

Acknowledgements

For permission to reprint the material in this book, the author and publisher would like to thank the following:

'Brief Confrontations': *The Crane Bag*, (Vol. 7, No.2, 1983); 'A Question of Imagination': *Cultural Contexts and Literary Idioms in Contemporary Irish Literature*, ed. Michael Kenneally (Colin Smythe, Gerrards Cross, 1988); 'An Absence of Influence': *Tradition and Influence in Anglo-Irish Poetry*, eds. Terence Brown and Nicholas Grene (Macmillan, London, 1989); 'Anatomist of Melancholia': *Honest Ulsterman* No. 73 (Louis MacNeice Number, September 1983); 'Against Piety': *The Poet's Place: Essays on Ulster Literature and Society*, eds. Gerald Dawe and John Wilson Foster (Institute of Irish Studies, Belfast, 1991); 'Our Secret Being': *Ruined Pages: Selected Padraic Fiacc*, eds. Gerald Dawe and Aodán MacPóilin (Blackstaff Press, Belfast, 1994); 'Blood and Family': *Studies in Contemporary Irish Literature*, ed. Michael Kenneally (Colin Smythe, Gerrards Cross, 1993); 'Invocation of Powers': *The Chosen Ground: Essays on Contemporary Poetry of Northern Ireland*, ed. Neil Corcoran (Seren Books, Mid-Glamorgan, 1992); "'And Then—the Spring!' Brendan Kennelly's *Breathing Spaces*": *Dark Fathers Into Light: Brendan Kennelly*, ed. Richard Pine (Bloodaxe Books, Newcastle upon Tyne, 1994); 'Icon and Lares': *Across a Roaring Hill: The Protestant Imagination in Modern Ireland*, eds. Gerald Dawe and Edna Longley (Blackstaff Press, Belfast, 1985); 'The Suburban Night': *Contemporary Irish Poetry: A Collection of Critical Essays*, ed. Elmer Andrews (Macmillan, London, 1992); 'Heroic Heart' is published for the first time in full.

Some of the material was originally presented in the form of lectures given under the auspices of Poetry Ireland (*An Absence of Influence*) and the John Hewitt International Summer School (*Against Piety*).

The author is grateful to Ms. Louise Kidney, Denis O'Brien, Damian Smyth, Jonathan Williams and The School of English, Trinity College, Dublin, for their help in preparing this book for publication.

ISBN: 1 873687 75 3
Author: Gerald Dawe
Title: Against Piety: Essays in Irish Poetry
1995

Front Cover: *Young Breton Girl* (1903) by Roderic O'Conor
(Courtesy of the Hugh Lane Gallery)
Cover Design by December Publications
Set in New Baskerville
Printed by Noel Murphy, Belfast

for Bridget O'Toole

Every good poem is very nearly a Utopia.
—W.H. Auden, *The Dyer's Hand*

CONTENTS

Preface

Some lines of poetry remain fixed in one's mind and they can surface at any time. Two poems have stayed with me in this way. They come from my years as a pupil at Orangefield Boys' School, Belfast during the mid-1960s. I can still hear the voice of my first teacher of English, Mr. Dai Francis, recite the General Prologue to *The Canterbury Tales,* as the class looked on, caught somewhere between awe and embarrassment:

> Whan that Aprille with his shoures sote
> The droghte of Marche hath perced to the rote,
> And bathed every veyne in swich licour
> Of which vertu engendred is the flour.

We would have been about 15 years old at the time.

The other set of lines are from the opening book of another great English poem:

> Him the Almighty Power
> Hurled headlong flaming from th' ethereal sky
> With hideous ruin and combustion down
> To bottomless perdition, there to dwell
> In adamantine chains and penal fire.

The voice this time is a very different teacher, Sam McCready, and he is putting the fifth and sixth years through a rehearsal of his dramatisation of Milton's *Paradise Lost.*

Orangefield was an extraordinary school, managed by John Malone in the heartland of east Belfast. I travelled weekdays across town from the frowsy lower middle-class north Belfast, meeting friends outside C&As or Robinson Cleaver's, before taking the bus through the stepped streets of working-class districts such as Albertbridge and the Newtownards Road. We were taught Keats and Shakespeare, Tennyson and Wilfred Owen. Our history was mostly military; our geography geological; our sense of who we were based exclusively on the city of Belfast that spread out before us like the palm of a hand. What

Chaucer or Milton had to do with this world raises many of the questions that have fascinated me ever since.

Belfast was a country all to itself, and everything we knew and experienced was seen through the eye of that needle.

I dare say this exclusive, insular confidence, so much a part of the mid-60s, was a fool's paradise, but it was out of that time that I discovered poetry. I lived in the Public Library, visited bookshops and eagerly read everything I could get my hands on. There were a couple of good bookshops around town, as well as our own *casbah* known as Smithfield, in which you could stumble upon just about any book imaginable. Two anthologies stand out though: Michael Roberts's *The Faber Book of Modern Verse*, and *The New Poetry*, edited by A. Alvarez. There was also the Penguin Modern Poets Series which had an almost cultic status—Akhmatova, Quasimodo, *Four Greek Poets* (Cavafy, Seferis, Elytis and Gatsos) and Vasko Popa.

Side by side with this life of books, there was the endless dancing, parties and concerts. I do not think anyone actually *went* anywhere, except, perhaps, for summer jobs to King's Lynn, Earl's Court or Guernsey. We did talk a lot, however; listened for what seemed like forever to R&B, blues and jazz. The club-life was vital and exciting.

In the back of my mind, though, there was always the desire to write. I had already written some woeful poems in school, recorded them in science notebooks alongside quotations from Albert Camus, Dostoyevsky, Yeats and Dylan Thomas. I showed the poems to a handful of friends, treating the whole thing like a terrible secret. Writing and poetry were deeply private, almost sacred, things to do, but there was also the nagging question: how could someone from my background actually write with any authority?

There was, along with the school books and the Penguins, several anthologies lying around the house which my grandmother had used for elocution classes. These books included the work of many English and American poets whose very different voices sounded more in keeping with what I took to be my own. Then, as if in an act of confirmation, in our final year at school, 1968, the poet and playwright Stewart Parker gave a special class in Orangefield at which he read the poems of Sylvia Plath. The shock was immediate and I will never forget it:

> There's a stake in your fat black heart

And the villagers never liked you.
They are dancing and stamping on you.
They always *knew* it was you.
Daddy, daddy, you bastard, I'm through.

And so my first really publishable poem was called 'I'm Through', although I had sent to Michael Longley, through the sister of a friend who was being taught by him, a poem called 'From This Time Without'. The poem was based upon Colin Blakely's performance in Denis Potter's television play, *The Son of Man.* Michael Longley's gracious advice about writing has withstood the test of time.

When I eventually went to college a couple of years after leaving school, I had behind me a lot of reading and a devotee's unwieldy sense of what literature meant. I also had a rather undisciplined idea that writing poetry, and writing *about* it, was what I wanted to do with my life. Indeed, that this was all I really could do.

After a somewhat circuitous route (London, hanging out in Belfast, applying for strange jobs such as 'Time and Motion' at Richardson's Mills, thinking about Guildhall or RADA, and finally being accepted as a 'cub' reporter at my great-grandfather's editorial home, the *Belfast Telegraph*), I finally started at the fledgling University of Ulster in 1971 with the novelist and critic Walter Allen as professor. I count myself lucky that a brilliant young lecturer and tutor, Bridget O'Toole, was also on the staff. Her knowledge of literature in English, matched by a passionate understanding of the political life of the imagination, introduced to a motley crew of northern Irish, Scottish and renegade English, the rigours of literary criticism and critical theory. Our hero was Walter Benjamin, the fugitive writer and intellectual.

Later on, Bridget O'Toole was joined by Bill McCormack, and, between them, my own understanding of Irish and European literature developed.

Against Piety is derived from the discussions we held, in tutorials and late night sessions, during the early 70s, in the unlikely setting of boarding rooms, rented flats and houses in what was then known, in local parlance, as The Triangle—Portstewart, Coleraine and Portrush. Also during this time at the University of Ulster, I discovered, through friends, literature in Irish, particularly Seán O Ríordáin's poetry.

Against the background of encroaching political violence and sectarianism in the north of Ireland, our own imaginative lives were formed. If I take a 'softer' view of the late 60s, it is probably because it was, relatively speaking, free from the terrible pressures that built up around people once the 'Troubles' spilled out into the streets. The big question was how to redress artistic desire with the very real and immediate social consequences of historical conflict, political failure and paramilitary violence.

I met Padraic Fiacc at this time. He was a link between the contradictory world of, on the one hand, Padraic Colum, Joyce and Beckett, and, on the other, the violent and hidden history of Belfast with, inbetween, the mediating figures of European writers such as Baudelaire, Mauriac and Pascal.

It is only with the hindsight of more than 20 years, however, that I realise the importance to me of one particular volume of poems published during this period. Derek Mahon's *Lives* (1972) got the balance just right between detachment (a curse on all your houses) and personal rage; cosmopolitan knowingness, shadowed by dark, local secrets. There was, too, the overriding integrity of Mahon's poetry which resisted, with its astringent self-mockery, the tried and tested formulae of the past.

When I left the north in October 1974, at a time of horrifying sectarian murders—with my family, friends, Belfast and the part of it where I had lived condemned in a way to the life of an occupied city—I took with me a battery of images which eventually would surface in my own poetry.

In the nature of things, it was probably no coincidence that I found myself in another coastal environment, Galway, on the western seaboard, where I settled for the next 20 years or so. It was during my years in Galway that I started to write about the cultural meshing that binds together poetry and history. I also started to mull over what keeps these human processes separate and distinct. This tension of attraction and repulsion is at the core of *Against Piety*.

It was my good fortune to find friends in Galway whose literary passions were close to my own. Since I never felt myself to be part of any specific group or regional identity, literature became the homeground. I published, along with contemporaries such as Harry Clifton, Gerard Fanning, Des Hogan, Neil Jordan and Ronan Sheehan, in *St.Stephen's*, the *UCD Broadsheet* and David Marcus's 'New Irish

Writing' in the *Irish Press.* I was lucky, too, in working at University College, Galway—first with Lorna Reynolds and, a little later, with the playwright and novelist Thomas Kilroy. It was during this time, in the late 70s, that I learned much from the critical writings of Seamus Deane.

I also involved myself in various writing schemes, from establishing the monthly literary supplement 'Writing in the West', published by the *Connacht Tribune,* to organising throughout the west of Ireland writers' workshops called 'Starting to Write'. I published my first book of poems, *Sheltering Places* (1978) and the first edition of an anthology of poetry, *The Younger Irish Poets* (1982).

I started to publish criticism and reviews and gave readings in various parts of Ireland which I had never been near, such as Kilkenny and Cork, and further afield, in Holland and France.

There was a kind of *naïveté* about such things then that has, probably inevitably, given way to the increased professionalisation and marketing of poetry in Ireland. The *naïveté* also extends to the arbitrariness with which I took up teaching. I still sometimes wake up in a cold sweat recalling my first class in 1977 on Keats's poetry, when I had enough material prepared for a semester instead of one hour.

I sleep-walked through much of the early 80s, living in, and writing about, the west of Ireland; learning about different styles of life and witnessing, too, the saga of the north as it unfolded before a bewildered Republic. That story proved to be emblematic, as I tried to tell family, close friends and colleagues. The crisis came for me in 1981 when the birth of our daughter crossed against the anguish of the grisly hunger strikes; living and dying in Ireland became a basic matter of choice.

Where I remembered the common ground of the pre-Troubles era and a determination, when the violence finally erupted, *not* to bow to history's grand imperatives, there was now a televised wasteland, a motorway link or a government policy decision on cultural traditions. My writing as a poet and critic went underground. I felt I had to rethink. I began to tap discarded energies and return to the freer, eclectic roots that I had known growing up in Belfast and during the dark days of the city before I left in 1974.

I also grew to despise the rhetoric of nationalism *and* unionism which no longer fitted into the realities of life in the Republic of Ireland or the Britain of the 80s.

With older European wounds reopening, the venerable liberal democracies looked as helpless before the force of history as poet and poetry were in countering the northern Irish turmoil and its cultural and political impact elsewhere. What had been happening in the north became part of the greater social and political landscape of our time. I also felt that these fault lines were the very souterrains of the poetry and fiction which I had been drawn to since the late 60s, from Auden and Montale to Camus and Kundera.

A poet who writes criticism cannot forget the people who make up his or her original audience. Many of the notions and attitudes brought into the writing of these essays first saw the light of day in class discussions, seminars and workshops conducted during the 80s. While *Against Piety* is not theoretically motivated, the underlying pattern of critical and intellectual bias should be sufficiently clear from my title. The argument is not with the past but with inherited uses (or abuses) of poetry and criticism in Ireland. To all those readers, writers and students, young and old, bored or bothered, committed, contrary or unconvinced; full-time, part-time, day-time and night-time, I offer my deepest thanks.

To the commissioning editors of the various books and journals where this material first appeared, I gratefully acknowledge their permission to reprint such work in *Against Piety*.

I have learned much from the incisive comments of my wife, Dorothea Melvin. She lived with the thinking-through of these essays while working in difficult circumstances on fundamental issues of women's health and social rights. Whatever coherence and resolution my writing has achieved owes much more than I can say to her consistent support.

Gerald Dawe
Dún Laoghaire
Co. Dublin
1994

1

Brief Confrontations

The Irish Writer's History

I want to begin with a quotation from the published extract from Thomas Kinsella's 1966 address to the Modern Languages Association in New York when, concluding his remarks on 'The Irish Writer', he stated:

> ... for the present—especially in this present—it seems that every writer has to make the imaginative grasp at identity for himself; and if he can find no means in his inheritance to suit him, he will have to start from scratch.[1]

The assumption that the writer is constitutionally free to 'start from scratch', that there are no ineradicable blemishes or scars, might appear too idealistic, but it marks an important demarcation in the deterministic vocabularies of 'influence', 'roots' and 'place', which occupy so much of the discussion about the nature of Irish poetry in the English language. The freedom, the *necessary* freedom Kinsella suggests, is for the writer to choose an imaginative identity and, if that identity is framed by an inappropriate tradition, then it is the writer's responsibility to create an alternative tradition that is liberating.

It is an awkward point summoning up those perpetual questions: to what extent is the writer truly free to create one's own tradition? How does a writer's own identity 'fit' into a tradition? What is a tradition—a home, a prison, a cave?

It seems to me that Kinsella answers these questions for himself in the 1966 address, but leaves the theoretical matter unresolved while, simultaneously, clearing the cluttered places of Irish history and myth to make space for his own creativity.

The questions re-emerge, however, when we consider the finished products of such creative moments: have they engaged things and places outside of themselves? Immediately, we are back in the treacherous seas of what literature is, what it means and how we can evaluate it.

I do not intend to tackle any of these issues directly. The aim of this essay is to consider the abstract creative moment and to define a few of the levers of power that are, in my mind, exerted upon it by what Thomas Kinsella calls 'inheritance'.

The concern is with process, the transformation that takes place on interacting levels between the past (as inheritance) and the present (as creative moment), and the expressive form this activity establishes as a literary convention.

Transformations, processes, changes are most difficult to define, presupposing a clear-sighted point at which we can identify something as it alters, modifies itself and becomes different. As historians have emphasised, 'dates' are signposts marking shifts and movements, imperceptible or overt, but rarely adequate for the complexity of what happened or is in the process of becoming.

It seems as if we are dumb before the Chinese box of history or that we must applaud Madame Guillotine as she rigidly exacts her meaning. Either way, we look like acquiescent adepts of hindsight, willing to accept what the past is with a troubled conscience that it is the Past, bearing down upon us in controllably subterranean ways while remaining, paradoxically, petrified. It is only when the past erupts in the present that it becomes more than rhetorical; its meaning is no longer assumed.

This paradox, which on a social level means conflict, exists as a lever of power in what I have vaguely called the creative moment, the present. Denis Donoghue, in *The Sewanee Review*, alluded to the problem when he wrote:

> ... it is my impression that Irish writers sense a rift between experience and meaning, but in reverse; the meaning is premature, already inscribed by a mythology they have no choice but to inherit, and the experience is too narrow to be entirely natural and representative.[2]

One can itemise this rift by referring to the terms which are generally used to describe 'Irish experience' but are shied away from on an intellectual level: Protestant/Catholic, worker/owner, male/female. Around these terms lie the experiences and mythologies out of which the writer works, imaginatively transcending, one hopes, their intransigent contradiction, but not reducing them either to sociological ascriptions or exploiting them merely in the interest of local colour. By referring to these terms, I do not want to prosecute a case for what is or is not 'relevant'. On the contrary, it is the claims of such terms, the ways in which they insidiously or oppressively govern the self, that need analysis. It is my belief that this can be achieved most effectively through works of the imagination. Yet there are several aspects of modern Irish poetry which suggest that such an analysis is resisted, that the literary tradition actively consorts *against* definition by promoting instead abstract strategies about 'the national identity', or more recently, 'regionalism', amongst other agendas.

One can read, for instance, much of the poetry found in the books, anthologies and magazines of the 20s and 30s in Ireland without having a clear sense that it has been written by individuals who feel and think, doubt and question. The poem, one suspects, writes itself. I experience this in the poetry of Padraic Colum and F.R. Higgins, for instance. In the guise of a seemingly non-literary language, the poem is contained within a fixed framework of response. Take Higgins's much anthologised poem, 'Father and Son':

> Yes, happy in Meath with me for a day
> He walked, taking stock of herds hid in their own breathing;
> And naming colts, gusty as wind, once steered by his hand,
> Lightnings winked in the eyes that were half shy in greeting
> Old friends—the wild blades, when he gallivanted the land.

What distinguishes this passage, with its stylised voice ('Yes, happy in Meath'), the inclusive metaphor ('colts, gusty as wind'), the colloquialism ('gallivanted') and the assumption of a compliant audience from, say, Colum's 'Plougher', is the muscular exhortation of the latter:

> Sunset and silence! A man; around him earth savage, earth broken;
> Beside him two horses, a plough!

Rather than exploring an unliterary language, what is happening in both these poems is, I think, a formalised literary use of language and the poet's acceptance of a convention which involves recurrent images and stock motifs.

This form of a 'literary language', as an inheritance, generally has been related to the rural bases of Irish history and mythology.

Irish poetry's dependence upon Nature as a source of metaphor has often been remarked upon.[3] Taken on a parallel level, one can see that much of modern Irish poetry has been descriptive, passively registering this dominant convention. As the social historian Michael D. Higgins has written, in another context,

> ... that writing which has drawn the most public attention has unfailingly been informed by nostalgia, or on occasion its variation, bitter memory. To jog the sensibilities into a critical self-appraisal has been dangerous at least. [4]

The critical self-appraisal referred to here has been obscured *precisely because* of the dominant poetic convention represented by figures such as Colum and F.R. Higgins. We can take this point one step further by considering the belief in a native Irish legacy, whereby language itself is viewed as inherently 'poetic' and its stock of images an open medium for rendering meaning. The poet merely dips in and draws forth 'poetry'. In Ireland, it seems, we have accepted this notion of a 'poetic language' and have consequently neglected the critical faculty. We have also accepted, by implication at least, a certain way of looking at the world as an infallible ordinance of predictability. The self is insufficient, so moral and political responsibilities are assumed by those who 'know better' and who, with this knowledge converted into power, control our world. The poetic language, the belief in such a thing, is a language of myth, sanctities and obligative truths[5], and it colludes with the conventionalised history of significant events: 1690, 1848, 1916. The meaning, as Denis Donoghue remarked, is premature; it is given, institutionalised, monolithic. The creative moment, the present, is swept aside, inundated with one version of the past, and with it the complex relationship of the self with the world it inhabits is trivialised. It is this relationship that Thomas Kinsella is referring to in the quotation at the opening of this essay, a relationship which he seeks in his own work to explicate, protect and free.

It would, of course, be foolish to assume that Higgins or Colum were consciously spokesmen for a dominant literary convention. It was Yeats, after all, who propagated that convention in modern Ireland. Yet he was master of it and this mastery was sustained by the peculiar power his imagination derived from the idea of an alternative tradition, one that he had 'built from scratch'.[6]

The idea of the 'noble and beggarman' enabled Yeats to dramatise conflicting sets of metaphors and their associated emotional, cultural and political states. The idea was, as Seamus Deane has shown[7], an untenuous historical fiction. John Hewitt formed an alternative tradition, less spectacular than Yeats's, but one substantiated by Hewitt's meticulous historical rediscovery of the Rhyming Weavers and their submerged artisan culture.[8]

It is significant that these poets (Yeats and Hewitt) are Protestant. I am using the terms 'Protestant' and 'Catholic' in the sense that they distinguish the access a writer may or may not have in Ireland to mythic and symbolic realities.[9]

It is an access which was more limited in the Protestant tradition or, to put this another way, the Protestant tradition in Ireland seemed less compatible to the artistic imagination, and consequently 'Protestant' writers like Yeats, Synge, Beckett and Hewitt made the constructing of an imaginative inheritance a substantial part of their literary identity and ambition, a priority which they, as individuals but in common, began 'from scratch'.[10]

Undoubtedly, both traditions can be limiting and restrictive to the individual writer who has been shaped by them. My point is that the Catholic writer has had a more direct, fluent and engaged relationship with the metaphoric and symbolic sources that cluster around the idea of an Irish poetic inheritance. To pretend otherwise glosses over important aspects of that inheritance. Thomas Kinsella's comment shows that his own scrupulous brooding on this theme anticipates a possible new departure (dated over 20 years ago). Going back to writers such as F.R. Higgins, we can see that his relationship as a Protestant to such sources was artificially constructed, lacking the conflict Yeats found through other imaginatively fertile perspectives such as the lure of Byzantium. Padraic Colum's poetry, on the other hand, reveals how easy it was (and still is) for a Catholic writer in Ireland to exploit the homiletic and complicit form of expression. This tendency Patrick Kavanagh was to debate with himself throughout his mature writing years. His response to what he finally came to see as the debasing notion of the Yeats-inspired 'peasant quality' deprived him, for a time at least, of absorbing the aesthetic design and composure of Yeats's poetry. Indeed, Kavanagh seemed to hesitate between different images of himself as a poet.

His earlier confidence in writing was drawn from the 'natural' place the figure of the poet had held in a rural community but, through his experience of Dublin literary society and the 'literariness' of its myth of 'the poet', Kavanagh needed to create for himself a more self-consciously literary identity. This he never consistently did, and the instability of his artistic achievement is the result.

In reacting against the discredited myth, though, Kavanagh also dismissed the poems he had written under its influence: "The Irish audience I came into contact with tried to draw out of me everything that was loud, journalistic and untrue."[11]

In 'The Hero', the ironic opening conceals, one suspects, the real uncertainties, echoing back to his experience of literary Dublin:

> He was an ordinary man, a man full of humour,
> Born for no high sacrifice, to be no marble god;
> But all the gods had failed that harvest and someone spread the rumour
> That he might be deluded into taking on the job.
> And they came to him in the spring
> And said: you are our poet-king.

Kavanagh's uncertainty about his identity as a poet may have been subsumed in the greater threat of illness to his life. The doubt remained: what was the authentic role and voice of the poet? How was he to strike out of such orthodoxies of a conventional 'poetic' language, and find his real voice?

Kavanagh's answers were, in part, negatives; he collapsed the argument by debunking 'art' and substituting the commonplace, the ordinary: "[to] wallow in the habitual, the banal,/grow with nature again as before I grew."

We are still dealing with that particular inheritance. Yet it is instructive to consider a similar process in the work of Padraic Fiacc, since he exhibits, like Kavanagh, a prejudice against the mythology of art and the poet. In Fiacc's poetry, however, the prejudice is obsessive, fed by what he sees as the disabling claims of Irish history and the dominating idioms of conventional Irish poetry. What is more, the ordinary and the commonplace are transformed in Fiacc's poetry by the recent events of Northern Ireland's history.

Fiacc's poem, 'Elegy in "The Holy Land"', is a good example of how he relates to the Irish past. Like many of his poems, 'Elegy ...' records Fiacc's disenchantment with the political, cultural and religious parlance that has shaped his identity as a poet. The poem sets itself against the idolising incantation of Mangan's 'Dark Rosaleen' with the latter's "my Queen,/ My life of life, my saint of saints", her "bright face" clouded like "the mournful moon". It is this woman, "at home ... in your emerald bowers", whose vision Mangan seeks to free:

> But yet ... will I rear your throne
> Again in golden sheen;
> 'Tis you shall reign, shall reign alone,
> My Dark Rosaleen!

As with other such poems, or *aislings*, the poet proclaims, with a barely concealed identification of the woman as Ireland, the inevitable sacrifice:

> O! the Erne shall run red
> With redundance of blood,
> The earth shall rock beneath our tread,
> And flames wrap hill and wood,
> And gun-peal, and slogan cry,
> Wake many a glen serene
> Ere you shall fade, ere you shall die,
> My Dark Rosaleen!

We are in the customary setting of one dominant inheritance—the blood sacrifice and the hope of eventual freedom rooted in struggle. The poem's conventional landscape underlies the reverence of its vision and is saved from maudlin sentimentality only by the forcefulness of lines like

> The Erne ... at its highest flood,
> I dashed across unseen,
> For there was lightning in my blood,
> My Dark Rosaleen!

Fiacc's poem takes this commentary as assumed: he writes directly out of the tradition in which a poem like 'Dark Rosaleen' would have the implicit emotional resonance of an immediately recognisable nostalgia of cherished ideals. Such a tradition still exists in Ireland, despite the attempts of political or cultural 'revisionists' to disarm it. Fiacc's poem seeks to confront it on a variety of levels. The form of 'Elegy ...' is disjunctive, undermining the audience's compliance; the landscape is urban and the vision has been transmogrified to a

Girl with the whooping cough
                    gliding
Through the wall-tall, caved-in
Cliffs of us being kids.

The sickly child is, nevertheless, part of an inherited vision, her identity as a "small unsmiling/self/With a doll's pram" is not lost but defined by "this/Black shame on us low/-land Scotch drunks call being alive". The ending of the poem distills the contradiction between vision and reality, an ending which sees the vision (in its rewritten form) as a legacy drawn from the persistent conventional metaphors of the Irish past:

O dolly-Eurydice, my dark Ros
-aleen dream
of bog on bog of bone
-grounded cloud, Ireland, my dear

Dragon seed pod ...

What Kavanagh and Fiacc have, nominally, in common is a sense of myth, inheritance and the past crumbling in the hands of their present. They express, on different imaginative levels, the "rift between experience and meaning", but with Fiacc this rift has become a condition of his own creativity, expressed formally in the shape and experience of the poetry itself. His has become a truly modern voice.

It seems, though, that the poetic convention Yeats propagated was maintained by poets like Higgins and Colum and subsequently reinvigorated by Kavanagh in his best-known poems, 'Epic', or 'Kerr's Ass', for example. Kavanagh tried, however, to redefine the convention to accord more with his own self-awareness and experience of Irish life. In style, technique, in form, Kavanagh updated the convention without actually transforming it. It continues to dominate Irish poetry.

In this reading, and given the testimony of contemporary poets such as John Montague and Seamus Heaney, Kavanagh stands as *the* most important figure in Irish poetry of the last three decades. His presence is continuously reaffirmed in the work of some of the finest younger poets writing in English, such as Paul Durcan and Paul Muldoon.

It is important, at this late stage, to state the obvious: the poets mentioned here are predominantly northern. It is not coincidental, surely, that recent years have seen substantial critical attention being paid to the idea of 'northern poetry'. The refined, expanded and more self-consciously literary work of these poets is directly linked to the inheritance and influence which Kavanagh's poetry and prose continues to exert.

It should also be apparent, given the currency of the term 'northern poetry', that poets like Louis MacNeice, Michael Longley, Derek Mahon and Tom Paulin are distanced from this inheritance. They often address it, but they do not speak out of it.

Consequently, it is surely an oversimplification to speak of 'northern poetry' as a homogeneous grouping prefixed by region and enfranchised by political or cultural proximities separate from the rest of the country. The imaginative 'initiative' has roamed more erratically and less conveniently than such an ascription would allow and seems to be asserting itself, on several different levels, in the terms of Kinsella's remarks on the Irish writer.

This is not, I think, a matter of speculation or of current fad, but rather a feeling for the basis of attempts being made to explore other facets of experience and imaginative ideals, such as one sees in the work of, say, Eavan Boland and Paul Durcan. Nor have I succumbed, I trust, to that process which John Berger commented upon when he wrote:

> I have come to see that the arranging of artists in a hierarchy of merit is an idle and essentially dilettante process. What matters are the needs which art answers.[12]

The 'needs' which Berger refers to are coexistent with an audience's 'expectations' of what a poem is, what it should deal with and in what form. In Ireland, as Michael D. Higgins suggests, writers (and particularly poets) have been especially conscious of these expectations. This consciousness has been double-edged: of accepting (or acquiescing in) formal conventions and of formally fulfilling needs and expectations. There is not, so far as I know, anything wrong with this. It has contributed to the popularity of poetry in Ireland over recent years, a consciousness that poetry is being written and that it is, in some manner of means, of importance. Precisely how it is important is left generously vague. Such a situation could, imperceptively but significantly, degenerate into a self-delighting but obedient wit. But I do not think this will happen. We have reached a point, possibly through the trauma of the late 70s and 80s, where the Irish past and the silted nets of convention are finally becoming untangled. More poets are unwilling to accept the pervasive experience of the past, without first questioning its relevance to them as creative individuals.

In concluding her introduction to Walter Benjamin's *Illuminations*, Hannah Arendt wrote:

> Any period to which its own past has become as questionable as it has to us must eventually come up against the phenomenon of language, for in it the past is contained ineradicably, thwarting all attempts to get rid of it once and for all.[13]

In that almost throwaway phrase, "the phenomenon of language", we are 'up against' the crucial unexplored theme of Irish writing: not in the sense of labyrinthine Heideggerian disclosures, nor in the linguistic minutiae of dialect studies. The phenomenon of language in Ireland takes us back to the semantics of strife and the seeds of historical disaffection which continue to threaten the individual imagination by overshadowing the range and validity of its perceptions. In this confrontation, brief and secretive and arbitrary as it often is, new ways of truth can be found and therein lies the poet's responsibility: something that is outside the literal conventions and orthodoxies of our literary past. As Czeslaw Milocz said:

> The creative act is associated with a feeling of freedom that is, in its turn, born in the struggle against an apparently invincible resistance.[14]

Notes

[1] Thomas Kinsella, 'The Irish Writer', in *Davis, Mangan, Ferguson? Tradition and the Irish Writer* (Dublin: Dolmen Press, 1970), p. 66.

[2] 'Being Irish Together', *The Sewanee Review*, Vol. LXXXIV, No. 1 (Winter 1976), p. 133.

[3] See, for instance, Seamus Heaney's 'The Sense of Place' in *Preoccupations: Selected Prose 1968-1978* (London: Faber & Faber, 1980).

[4] M.D. Higgins, 'Liam O'Flaherty and Peadar O'Donnell: Images of Rural Community? The Location of some issues in the Sociology of Literature', unpublished paper read at the University of Hull, 1977.

[5] Hannah Arendt, 'Introduction: Walter Benjamin 1892-1940' in Benjamin's *Illuminations: Essays and Reflections* (London: Cape, 1970), p. 40.

[6] W.B. Yeats, 'The Municipal Gallery Revisited', *Collected Poems of W.B. Yeats* (London: Macmillan, 1969), p. 369.

[7] Seamus Deane, 'The Literary Myths of The Revival: A Case for their Abandonment', in *Myth and Reality in Irish Literature*, ed. Joseph Ronsley (Waterloo, Ontario: Wilfrid Laurier University Press, 1977).

[8] John Hewitt's *Rhyming Weavers* (Belfast: Blackstaff Press, 1974).

[9] See Hewitt's poem 'The Scar', where the two traditions interact as "that chance meeting/ That brief confrontation". *The Selected John Hewitt* (Belfast: Blackstaff Press, 1981), p. 26.

[10] The fact that a popular Protestant tradition of ballad and folk art still thrives does not undermine, I think, the specifically literary context of my argument.

[11] Patrick Kavanagh, *Collected Pruse* (London: Martin Brian & O'Keeffe, 1973), p. 16.

[12] John Berger, *Art and Revolution* (London: Writer & Readers Co-op, 1969), prefacing note.

[13] *Illuminations*, p. 49.

[14] Czeslaw Milosz, *The Captive Mind* (Harmondsworth: Penguin Books, 1980), p. 217.

2

A Question of Imagination

Poetry in Ireland

I

My main concern here is with the public face of poetry in Ireland rather than with a specific analysis of this poet or that poem. It is doubtful if one can ever really separate the two, so that, in discussing their relatedness, I hope to show how a poet's identity as a poet is influenced by several literary, cultural and social assumptions about what poetry is and what 'being a poet' means.

I am mindful of the dangers in approaching my subject in this way—the poem can evaporate into an abstract poetry, and there is also the pitfall to which the Russian poet and critic Osip Mandelstam referred in his essay of 1922, 'On the Nature of the Word':

> If one listens to literary historians who defend evolutionism, it would appear that writers only think about how to clear the road for their successors, but never about how to accomplish their own tasks; or it would appear that they are all participants in an inventor's competition for the improvement of some literary machine, although none of them knows the whereabouts of the judges or what purposes the machine serves.[1]

One needs to be wary of this 'theory', which Mandelstam justifiably calls "the crudest, most repugnant form of academic ignorance". He describes its failure in the following terms:

> In literature nothing is ever 'better', no progress can be made simply because there is no literary machine and no finish line toward which everyone must race as rapidly as possible. This meaningless theory of

improvement is not even applicable to the style and form of the individual writer, for here as well, each gain is accompanied by a loss or forfeit.

So while there is, as Mandelstam maintains, no inevitable progress in literature, it is fair to say that various conventions and pressures can get in the way, restricting and weakening the integrity of poets and poetry to accomplish their fullest potential. I would like to concentrate upon one of these factors: the thematic bias of much contemporary poetry in Ireland.

I mean by thematic bias those clichés of history through which poetry is both written and read in Ireland. The persistent concern with 'identity', for instance, strikes me as being most characteristic of the recent period; of brooding upon what 'Irishness' means and what it does not. Poetry is taken as a central means towards negotiating this definition in, for example, its celebration of Irish landscape, or in the conveyancing of that landscape through the Irish language into the poetic forms of English. Uniting both points is the pervasive assumption that history is a terrible home for all Irish poets, the nightmare from which they must escape, like the archetypal artist-figure Stephen Dedalus. Feeding into this convention are various influences, one of the most important of which is that we have a *naturally* poetic language, because of the once central influence of the Irish language upon English as it is spoken in the country outside Dublin. While this may well be true in regard to common speech, it is essential to state the obvious here: that whatever benefits a poet can make out of this rich linguistic resource, they will not amount to much unless the poet possesses the necessarily imaginative rigour to use them effectively.

Flannery O'Connor's remarks are appropriate here, when addressing a Southern American Writers' Conference on "the gifts of the region"—speech, contrast, irony and contradiction:

> ... you [may] have seen these gifts abused so often that you have become self-conscious about using them. There is nothing worse than the writer who doesn't use the gifts of the region, but wallows in them.[2]

In Ireland, it is possible to relate this question to the way in which 'poetic' language is itself seen as a natural refuge, or homeplace, for the poet. Language becomes a message from history which the poet receives and transcribes through the medium of vowel, consonant and assonance:

> The tawny guttural water
> spells itself: Moyola
> is its own score and consort,
>
> bedding the locale
> in the utterance,
> reed music, an old chanter
>
> breathing its mists
> through vowels and history.
> A swollen river,
>
> a mating call of sound
> rises to pleasure me, Dives,
> hoarder of common ground.[3]

The colloquialism of idiom and image becomes an eloquent defining point of the poetry, and not the other way around. The pivotal metaphorical figure is in a place-name (Moyola) and, clustered around it, the images gather from Nature (the river), its voice (reed music) and the traditional Irish musical instrument (the uilleann pipes) into a summarising of "vowels and history" and the completion of "pleasure" for the rich man, Dives, "hoarder of common ground". These cyphers of meaning become rhetorical and the sentiment conventional in the hands of lesser poets than Seamus Heaney.

Literary precedence can be found, as Daniel Hoffman has remarked, in Yeats and latter-day Romanticism, where

> ... local-color writing celebrated the individualities of particular places, and gloried in whatever dialectical speech or surviving antiquities of custom or belief could be offered to prove the uniqueness of life in a given locality. Such a course, while risking quaintness, could put into a writer's hands ancient traditions as yet untouched by the mechanical forces of change since the Industrial Revolution. But in Ireland the impetus towards the literary uses of such material was not only from Romantic nostalgia. From the beginnings, the local-color movement had an overt political significance.[4]

The present risk is thematic predictability, with poetry losing out to a liturgical nostalgia which, in the end, serves "political significance".[5] Men and their physical environments recede into the folklore of locale and placenames.[6] Or, to paraphrase the German poet Heine, poetry is lost in "green lies", susceptible to the "fake greenishness" of landscape poetry.[7]

II

In a very useful review of new poetry in the English literary magazine *Stand*, Terry Eagleton referred to the "paradigm poem" and, giving an example from Paul Muldoon's *Quoof*, went on to say:

> ... the poem trades entirely on the intrinsic interest of its materials rather than on any imaginative transformation it submits them to. It is sentimentalism to believe that memories are valuable in themselves. To the writer of regional memories it is often enough a way of evading struggle with meaning, for such lovingly preserved experiences seem deceptively meaningful in themselves, and the act of narrating them assumes an auratic significance for which it has not sufficiently paid.[8]

The significance which Eagleton is scrutinising here comes from, in his estimation, an assumption that "the close rendering of an experience is somehow *inherently* meaningful; and this assumption survives only because the urban English reader will tend to collude with it, believing that an experience remote from him/herself—milking a cow, confronting the B-specials—is somehow more inherently significant than one more routinely familiar". Eagleton approaches this relationship of experience and language from another angle, when he writes in *Literary Theory: An Introduction* that if we

> ... understand the 'intentions' of a piece of language, we interpret it as being in some sense *oriented*, structured to achieve certain effects; and none of this can be grasped apart from the practical conditions in which the language operates. It is to see language as a practice rather than as an object; and there are of course no practices without human subjects.[9]

This is a most convincing argument and, when applied to Irish poetry, it is interesting to note that one of the more discernible trends is away from the use of language as practice, towards viewing language in a static sense, as a sacred object. The poet communes with and through language to form an abstract and rhetorical recognition out of his/her own poetic consciousness. It is in Tom Paulin's "voicing the word *nation*".

I'm tense now: talk of sharing power,
prophecies of civil war,
new reasons for a secular
mode of voicing the word *nation*
set us on edge, this generation,
and force the poet to play traitor
or act the half-sure legislator.[10]

It is in John Montague's naming of places:

and we leave, waving
a plume of black smoke
over the rushy meadows
small hills & hidden villages —
Beragh, Carrickmore,

Pomeroy, Fintona —
placenames that sigh
like a pressed melodeon
across this forgotten
Northern landscape.[11]

Seamus Heaney's work is generally acknowledged for the exemplary nature of precisely this kind of poetic consciousness. Take 'Anahorish' for example:

Anahorish, soft gradient
of consonant, vowel-meadow,

after-image of lamps
swung through the yards
on winter evenings.
With pails and barrows

those mound-dwellers
go waist-deep in mist
to break the light ice
at wells and dunghills.[12]

This is a perfect illustration of the way *one* central theme in Heaney's poetry marks out language as an object and of how the poet defines his self and his past in that special pastoral awareness of his own place through a metaphorical appropriation of its idiom.[13] Heaney's *Station Island*[14] shifts this preoccupation on to those occasions, real and imagined, when the poet succumbs to the poetry-making, as in 'The Loaning' ("I knew/I was in the limbo of lost words") or in 'Making Strange':

> I found myself driving the stranger
>
> through my own country, adept
> at dialect, reciting my pride
> in all that I knew, that began to make strange
> at that same recitation.[15]

Heaney's poems consolidate this process of treating language as an object, in that he considers his relation to the very experiences he is writing about *as a poet.* The sequence 'Station Island' seeks to sort out an appropriate place for the poet—one that is adequate both to the world he presently inhabits and the world of his past. My own reading of *Station Island* is that the book represents this particular poetic self-consciousness as confining. It makes Heaney concentrate much more upon the fact that he is writing, rather than upon what he is actually writing about. Perhaps this is the likely result, if we bear in mind the perspective that Terry Eagleton offers in the above quotations. For if language becomes an object in the poet's hands, the occasion of his writing will be viewed with equal importance, and, by its very literariness, this focuses on the poet and the personality of his or her own artistic self in relaying the poem to us:

> Then I sat there writing, imagining in silence
> sounds like love sounds after long abstinence,
> eager and absorbed and capable
> under the sign of a snowshoe on a wall.
>
> The loop of the snowshoe, like an old-time kite,
> lifts away in a wind and is lost to sight.
> Now I sit blank as gradual morning brightens
> its distancing, inviolate expanse.[16]

It is on these three themes that much of the attention given to Irish poetry is centred. The critical perspectives converge upon where the poet fits into public debate (Paulin's "prophecies of civil war"), the delineation of nostalgic landscapes of home (Montague's "small hills & hidden villages") and the sense of being a poet in the first place (Heaney's "I sat there writing, imagining in silence").

In Ireland, too, there is a widely held perception of the poet as some kind of public figure who, in regard to both his social life and beliefs, voices on behalf of 'the people' an accessible articulation of their spiritual and cultural beliefs. This stereotypical image of the poet as a public figure is possibly derived from the populist context in which Irish poetry in English first developed, from the mid-19th to the early part of the 20th century. However, the fact there are now dramatically-changed social and cultural conditions, wherein complex and contradictory ideals conflict, does not seem to have substantially altered this perception of the poet. It may well be another remnant of that Romantic idealism to which Daniel Hoffman refers; in this instance, of seeing the poet as a sensitive soul, damaged at birth by a fragmented inheritance, bearing artistically the scars of an inadequate Irish cultural milieu. A failure, in other words, not of our own making, but of England's; their language, imposed on ours; their culture forced upon us.

This conventional and normative view still obtains in Ireland, and poetry internalises the vision, transforming it into an acceptable myth which sustains the generally accepted cultural and politico-religious dogmas of modern Ireland.[17] As Seán Ó Faoláin remarked in *The Irish*, Irish writers from about "1890 to about 1940 ... saw Irish life, in the main, romantically. It was as a poetic people that they first introduced themselves to the world, and it is as a poetic poeple that they are still mainly known abroad".[18]

Poetry itself continues to be seen in this light, both in Ireland and elsewhere, as not so much imaginatively questioning reality, but rather in *naturalising* the traditional and inherited ways of reading it. This attitude may well come from the political nature of Irish life, where a homogeneous cultural nationalism holds sway and is mediated through the established images and modes of writing.

It is noticeable then that, given the crisis-prone history of present-day Ireland, with the proverbial emphasis on 'identity', traditional roles have asserted themselves in the poet's own work and the audience's expectations of that work. This conformity is an illustration of how generally acceptable that tradition is to poets. An artistic need to challenge it often occurs in poets who endeavour to examine those aspects of freedom (personal as much as social) which are available to them in the context of the literary and historical conditions of modern Ireland. For example, Thomas Kinsella's 'Nightwalker' retains its sharp critical edge and relevance as a major exploration of modern Irish experience and feeling:

> The officials on the corridors or in their rooms
> Work, or overwork, with mixed motives
> Or none. We dwell together in urgency;
> Dominate, entering middle age; subserve,
> Aborting vague tendencies with buttery smiles.
> Among us, behind locked doors, the ministers
> Are working, with a sureness of touch found early
> In the nation's birth—the blood of enemies
> And brothers dried on their hide long ago.
> Dragon old men, upright and stately and blind,
> Or shuffling in the corridor finding a key,
> Their youth cannot die in them; it will be found
> Beating with violence when their bodies rot.[19]

Kinsella's solitary anticipation of the issue of 'identity', which governs so much of the current discussion about literature and Ireland, well repays attention today. In his 1966 address to the Modern Languages Association in New York, for instance, he states:

> It is not as though literature, or national life, were a corporate, national investigation of a corporate national experience—as though a nation were a single animal, with one complex artistic feeler.[20]

In stating this basic fact, Kinsella also picked out the essential condition of any poet writing today:

> ... every writer in the modern world—since he can't be in all the literary traditions at once—is the inheritor of a gapped, discontinuous, polyglot tradition. Nevertheless, if the function of tradition is to link us living with the significant past, this is done as well by a broken tradition as by a whole one.

It is the imaginative exploration of this condition that distinguishes the best of Kinsella's poems, as it is with the poetry of Derek Mahon. His poetry, it can be said, composes that "gapped, discontinuous, polyglot tradition" to which Kinsella alludes. For Mahon brings into creative alignment with our own time a whole range of writers from Brecht and Pasternak to Gerard de Nerval, and his particular accomplishment has been the way he has discovered a *poetic* voice to achieve these new imaginative perspectives. It is a poetry of manner, highly tense yet balanced, and formally set within the conditions of definite times and places, but ineluctably leading out of these to wider questions, thoughts and feelings. By its very composure, Mahon's austerity of language rebukes sentimentality and denies any appeal to rhetoric. This incontrovertible restraint energises the poetry, drawing its forcefulness from the poet speaking his mind:

> When I returned one year ago
> I felt like Tonio Kröger—slow
> To come to terms with my own past
> Yet knowing I could never cast
> Aside the things that made me what,
> For better or worse, I am. The upshot?
> Chaos and instability.
> The cool gaze of the RUC.[21]

Feelings here are held in reserve, as a private matter mostly, but the actual world, which is being scrutinised in a dynamic way, includes the poet's sense of himself. This form of imaginative address can, in turn, be contrasted with the substantive formal disintegration one finds in the poetry of Padraic Fiacc.[22] Ironically, at a time when extensive discussion surrounds Irish literature, of how it relates to history and how the present crises have challenged the poet's imagination, Fiacc is rarely mentioned. Yet his work, on every conceivable artistic level of style and content, records the collapse of a society, its past and the nature of its contradictory ideals. Perhaps one reason for this failure of criticism relates to the kind of traditional relationship which exists between an Irish (or British) poet and his audience. Fiacc's poetry mocks this relationship and brings seriously into question the poet's place as regards a society (like Northern Ireland's) which lurches from crisis to crisis. It is a poetry that has little in common with the well-intentioned decorum which underlies the following comment from the introduction to *The Penguin Book of Contemporary British Poetry*:

> It is interesting to speculate on the relationship between the resurgence of Northern Irish writing and the Troubles. The poets have all experienced a sense of 'living in important places' and have been under considerable pressure to 'respond'. They have been brought hard up against questions about the relationship between art and politics, between the private and the public, between conscious 'making' and intuitive 'inspiration'. But on the whole they have avoided a poetry of directly documentary reportage.[23]

Speculations apart, Fiacc's poems have, for the past three decades, carried the marks of disaffection, prejudice and hope that are embedded in ordinary Northern Irish speech and idiom, and have formally and experimentally balanced the conscious 'making', the intuitive 'inspiration' *with* a poetry of 'directly documentary reportage'. Perhaps Fiacc's position is explicable in similar terms to Raymond Williams's remark about Thomas Hardy being "very disturbing for someone trying to rationalise refined, civilised, balancing judgment. Hardy exposes so much that cannot be displaced from its social situation, particularly in the later books".[24] Indeed Fiacc's later work, in particular, sympathetically and critically explores the social, cultural and religious situation and the illusions fostered by both sides in the northern conflict. This makes an exceptional witness out of his poetry, rather than making it a testament to "living in important places".[25] His poetry is important precisely because it *revokes* those very notions, and assumptions that I have looked at earlier in this essay, by subverting them and leaving in their place little by way of *traditional* aesthetic consolation. Instead, we find a harrowing act of imaginative redemption or an image bordering on what is grotesquely, comically human. Fiacc's poem 'The Wearing of the Black', for instance, mediates between the formal family scene of himself as a boy, "like the Prince of Wales", listening to his mother playing the piano, and the knowledgeable background of his father "*gone to America for/He is on the bloody run!*" The recollected music of 'See the Conquering Hero Comes' and 'The Bluebells of Scotland' gives way, as the awkward young boy drops a porcelain teacup:

> Now, near half a century after, why
> Can I recall that flash of fire on the tile

Floor as I scalded my bare knees when I pray
To care even that this rotting self-dinner

-jacketed hero's grave, tonight, in black cuff

Links, at least has the wit to dress for death.[26]

The clash between these two worlds of the past and present is characteristic of Fiacc's poetry, as is the culminating wry portrait that links both worlds in a new and disturbing perspective. It is as if nothing ever changes, only our ability to remember. The 'political situation', as Milan Kundera reminds us, "has brutally illuminated the ordinary metaphysical problem of forgetting that we face all the time, every day, without paying any attention. Politics unmasks the metaphysics of private life, private life unmasks the metaphysics of politics".[27] Possibly another reason for Fiacc's neglect is that his poetry unceasingly reasserts the unpalatable truthfulness of Kundera's statement. Indeed there is a 'political' consciousness in Fiacc's poetry, an appropriate rhetoric, which brings his work much closer to European and American models than it is to English poetry. This only further underlines his comparative isolation as a strangely modernistic voice, while he completes his 'Missa Terribilis' in the form of a traditional Mass.[28]

The poetry of Padraic Fiacc, Thomas Kinsella and Derek Mahon, as well as some of their younger contemporaries such as Paul Durcan, demonstrates a relative freedom from the kind of public conformations and conventions that I have noted briefly in the poetry of John Montague, Seamus Heaney and Tom Paulin. The poetic fruits of this freedom are found in the poet's own ironic, *critical* and questioning relationship with the details of his individual experience, feelings and ideas, and of how rigorously these are probed in and through the poetry. This is a valuable, if sometimes obscured, development: an imaginative negotiation that takes into account the Ireland we actually live in and the image poetry presents of it, along with all the other things that a poet needs to imagine.

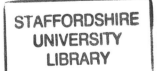

Notes

[1] Osip Mandelstam, *The Complete Critical Prose and Letters*, ed. J.G. Harris (Ann Arbour, Michigan: Ardis, 1979), p. 119.

[2] Flannery O'Connor, 'Writing Short Stories', in *Mystery and Manners: Occasional Prose* (London: Faber and Faber, 1972), p. 104.

[3] Seamus Heaney, 'Gifts of Rain: IV', *Wintering Out* (London: Faber and Faber, 1972), p. 25.

[4] Daniel Hoffman, *Barbarous Knowledge: Myth in the Poetry of Yeats, Graves and Muir* (London: Oxford University Press, 1970), p. 21.

[5] cf. Raymond Williams's remark, "Nostalgia, it can be said, is universal and persistent: only other men's nostalgias offend", in *The Country and the City* (London: Paladin, 1975), p. 21.

[6] See Brian Torode's 'Ireland the Terrible', in *Culture and Ideology in Ireland*, eds. Curtin, Kelly and O'Dowd (Galway: Galway University Press, 1984), pp. 20-29.

[7] Heine, *Die Bader von Lucca*, in H.H. Samtliche Werke, ed. Hans Kaufman (Munich: Kindler Verlag, 1964), Vol. V, pp. 234-44. I am indebted to Dr. Eoin Bourke of the German Department, University College, Galway, for this reference.

[8] Terry Eagleton, 'New Poetry', in *Stand Magazine*, 25, No. 3 (Summer 1984), pp. 76-80.

[9] Terry Eagleton, *Literary Theory: An Introduction* (Oxford: Basil Blackwell, 1983), p. 114.

[10] Tom Paulin, 'A Nation, Yet Again', *Liberty Tree* (London: Faber and Faber, 1983), p. 45.

[11] John Montague, 'Last Journey', *The Dead Kingdom* (Belfast: Blackstaff Press; Dublin: Dolmen Press, 1984), pp. 74-75.

[12] Seamus Heaney, 'Anahorish', *Wintering Out*, p. 16.

[13] A useful comparison can be made with Derek Walcott's *Midsummer* (London: Faber and Faber, 1984).

[14] Seamus Heaney, *Station Island* (London: Faber and Faber, 1984).

[15] ibid., pp. 32-33 (my italics).

[16] ibid., p. 24.

[17] I have looked at this viewpoint elsewhere: 'A Question of Convenants: Modern Irish Poetry', *The Crane Bag*, 3, No. 2 (1979); 'Checkpoints: The Younger Irish Poets', *The Crane Bag*, 6, No. 1 (1982); 'Convention as Conservatism', *The Crane Bag*, 7, No. 2 (1984); 'Poetry and the Public: Solitude and Participation', *The Crane Bag*, 8, No. 2 (1984); and 'The Permanent City: The Younger Irish Poets', in *The Irish Writer and the City*, ed. Maurice Harmon (Gerrards Cross: Colin Smythe; Totowa, New Jersey: Barnes & Noble, 1984), pp. 180-90.

[18] Seán Ó Faoláin, *The Irish* (Harmondsworth, Middlesex: Penguin Books, 1969), p. 143.

[19] Thomas Kinsella, 'Nightwalker', *Poems 1956-1973* (Dublin: Dolmen Press, 1980), p. 105.

[20] Thomas Kinsella, 'The Irish Writer', in *Davis, Mangan, Ferguson? Tradition and the*

Irish Writer (Dublin: Dolmen Press, 1970), p. 66.

21 Derek Mahon, 'The Sea in Winter', *Poems 1962-1978* (London: Oxford University Press, 1979), p. 111.

22 Padraic Fiacc's books include: *By the Black Stream: Selected Poems 1947-1967* (Dublin: Dolmen Press, 1969); *Odour of Blood* (Newbridge, Co. Kildare: The Goldsmith Press, 1973, reprinted 1984); *Nights in the Bad Place* (Belfast: Blackstaff Press, 1977); *The Selected Padraic Fiacc* (Belfast: Blackstaff Press, 1979).

23 Blake Morrison and Andrew Motion (eds.), *The Penguin Book of Contemporary British Poetry* (Harmondsworth, Middlesex: Penguin Books, 1982), p. 16.

24 Raymond Williams, *Politics and Letters: Interviews with New Left Review* (London: N.L.B. Verso ed., 1981), p. 246.

25 Damian Gorman pertinently remarks on this matter: "... part of the reason why so many of our local poets are so well known across the water is that this is a troubled region, deserving media attention. Thus poets are to some degree indebted to the situation. Our most urgent trouble at present is a complete lack of political imagination. It seems to me that men and women of poetic imagination might make a greater contribution to those reserves of communalty which will be needed to spirit us out of a state of attrition." 'Does Poetry Matter in Northern Ireland?', *Fortnight: An Independent Review for Northern Ireland*, No. 217 (April, 1985), p. 19.

26 Padraic Fiacc, *Nights in the Bad Place*, p. 37.

27 Milan Kundera, 'Afterwood: A Talk with the Author by Philip Roth', in *The Book of Laughter and Forgetting* (Harmondsworth, Middlesex: Penguin Books, 1983), p. 235.

28 'Missa Terribilis: A Sequence', *Paris/Atlantic; An Irish Issue* (American College in Paris, Paris, Summer 1985), subsequently collected in *Missa Terribilis* (Belfast: Blackstaff Press, 1986).

3

An Absence of Influence

Three Modernist Poets

Unlike statues, monuments, battle-sites or names of streets, a poetic tradition makes its presence felt in precariously obscure and intangible ways. In this essay, I will be drawing attention to the way we construct 'tradition' by considering the relationship to it of three important Irish poets—Brian Coffey, Denis Devlin and Thomas Kinsella. I want to consider why these poets exert such an ambivalent influence upon the general and critical perceptions about what constitutes the tradition of Irish poetry. Seamus Deane, in an essay on Derek Mahon entitled 'Freedom from History', has neatly summarised my approach when referring to Denis Devlin and Seán Ó Faoláin:

> For them, the cultivation of the intellect is not only a goal in itself but also a means of escape from besieged and rancorous origins. Others—Joyce, Beckett, Francis Stuart, Louis MacNeice—although they also seek in the world beyond an alternative to their native culture, have come to regard their exile from it as a generic feature of the artist's rootless plight rather than a specifically Irish form of alienation.[1]

Much of my essay relates to this qualified sense of exile and, in particular, to its creative bearing upon the kind of a poem a poet will write, as well as the critical context in which that poem will eventually find a place. I do not intend to look at the biographical sources of exile in the work of these poets, save where it touches directly upon a specific poem. Exile is, for present purposes, a useful metaphor of artistic space which embraces a spectrum of experience—in the case of Brian Coffey, an involuntary but nevertheless real condition; in the case of Denis Devlin, a feature of his life as a diplomat, but also a crucial feature of his imagination. With Thomas Kinsella, one cannot speak of exile so much as of a sense of isolation that is registered at a fundamental level in the poetry itself, and also in what he has said about poetry in Ireland. All three poets record in their work a reaction against the generally dominant scales of Irish poetry.

We encounter particularly important factors in the poetry of Coffey, Devlin and Kinsella: a sense of critical distance between their writing and the tradition; and the life of the intelligence, to which Seamus Deane alludes, is seen as an imaginative source for their poetry. By discussing their poems, the works of the imagination, as they are shaped beyond themselves into a poetic tradition, we are implicitly engaged, through a most complicated network, with the way poets, readers and everyone else for that matter, *create* that tradition in the first place.

Conservatism is one of the most significant features of the Irish poetic inheritance. This tradition, while being generally perceived as a fitting and copious home for poets, turns out under examination to be a limited one in many ways. James Mays has persuasively argued, in his essay introducing a special issue of the *Irish University Review* on Brian Coffey's poems, that "to dismiss a writer's claim to be considered on his own terms in favour of assigning him a role in a predetermined scheme"[2] bears directly upon that 'predetermined scheme' itself—namely, the Irish literary tradition.

How this tradition is contemporaneously articulated, in the literary media for instance, may lead a poet such as Denis Devlin to his early experiments in the 1930s with surrealism and his unfulfilled project to edit and translate into Irish an anthology of poems from the French. More customarily, the so-called poetic tradition establishes an order from the past, involving both an imperative and a selective rationalisation of all that has gone before. In this way, we invent traditions and the bases for these inventions are political as much as aesthetic, social as much as poetic. Rather like exceptions, exclusions confirm the rule.

Ironically, this tradition or scheme, with its ideals and priorities, was mainly established by Yeats, and we continue, even if in reaction, to accept the terms of reference he laid down. This is a pedagogical consolation and helps categorise writers like Austin Clarke and Patrick Kavanagh into chessboard-like relationships. What it ignores is the fundamental act of self-definition which every poet must experience, and the imaginative, critical and political distance this act may involve, between his or herself and the poetic tradition present at the time he or she is writing. Often this tradition will be seen as broken, inadequate, lifeless, stultifying, and the poet looks elsewhere to discover, not so much that which is new, but rather other forms and ideals which have meaning for him. This act of self-definition and the artistic consciousness which goes with it are central to the work of Coffey, Devlin and Kinsella *because* it implicates them in a reworking of the tradition, in the creation of an imaginative space beyond it.

Let me turn first to some of Brian Coffey's poems to describe in a more concrete fashion what I have been saying so far.

Perhaps one of Coffey's best-known poems is 'Missouri Sequence'. It is, among other concerns, a meditation on the meaning of 'home' and exile from such a place. The poem has been called Coffey's "most ambitious and successful to date".[3] It is traditional in a way that much of his poetry is not, explicitly and directly considering the poet's personal fate in a free, almost conversational form.

The four sections of the poem revolve around the necessity for Coffey to pull up his own and his family's roots in the United States and leave. Poetry becomes the counter registering the subtle shifts in feeling and idea as Coffey seeks to define the life he is leading:

> Tonight the poetry is in the children's game:
> I am distracted by comparisons,
> Ireland across the grey ocean,
> here, across the wide river.[4]

The opening section, 'Nightfall, Midwinter, Missouri', from which these lines come, is dedicated to Thomas MacGreevy, and it is to his old friend and fellow-poet that the poet speaks. Coffey looks at the different places where he has lived, starting with Ireland, before paraphrasing his feelings about England and France:

> ... I am charmed
> by the hills behind Dublin,
> those white stone cottages,
> grass green as no other green is green,
> my mother's people, their ways.

In case this conversational tone should falter into sentimentality, Coffey draws the connection between his fond remembrances and their actual personal effects:

> there is a love of Ireland
> withering for Irishmen.
>
> Does it matter where one dies,
> supposing one knows how?

Then, addressing MacGreevy, the poet asserts:

> Dear Tom, in Ireland,
> you have known
> the pain between
> its fruiting and the early dream
> and you will hear me out.

'Missouri Sequence' is a working out of two sides of the same question contained within these lines: "Does it matter where one dies". This question summons up the issue of 'home', of being amongst the people one knows, availing of that piety and its restrictions, while the 'pain' at the early dream of a truly independent Ireland implies disillusionment and failure. So Coffey is, in a sense, torn between the separated world that he *made* for himself and family (the created home in the United States) as against the world he knows in Ireland. They are both real worlds but also *ideas*, about the past and present; about the living and the dead; about struggle and passivity. The poet's life in the poem is suspended as if between both worlds, seeing through them, as it were, to what these contrary states of existence tell him about life itself and the one essential place where he discovers it flourishing—love:

> No servant, the muse
> abides in truth,
> permits the use of protest
> as a second best
> to make clean fields,
> exults only in the actual
> expression of a love,
> love all problem,
> wisdom lacking.

If 'Missouri Sequence' meditates on these themes, the source of the poem is straightforward. "Yet we must leave America", the poet states, and later in the marvellous concluding section, 'Missouri, Midsummer, Closure', he refers to the context of this decision:

> if I am victim,
> as I judge, of men
> who owed me respect.
>
> Useless, useless it is
> to ask what was done:
> celtic anger ruined me.
> Busy men see
> what it profits to see ...

The self is held up here to examination, but no bitterness mars the flow of its expression as poetry. The poetry is the main thing; not discontentment.

Coffey's continual, if 'accidental and non-deliberate', move away from Ireland is in effect anticipated in many of his early poems from the 30s. They are full of dramatised references to, and depictions of, sea-journeys, voyages and moments prior to departure. With titles like 'The Navigator', 'Quay', or the following questioning lines from 'Plain Speech for Two'[5], we have the impression of a constant restlessness and unease:

> And do you think he'd come back
> If he could
> or have you understood
> his sails are set on a new tack.

Somewhat earlier, in February 1933, Brian Coffey published in Paris *Three Poems*, the first of which is called 'Exile'. The scene is a remembered one, the recalled moment of walking a familiar street and seeing in his mind's eye a known landscape, while the present intervenes, cutting across Coffey's self-awareness:

> There, down the valley where the morning strode,
> The trees are interwoven tapestries
> In purples that illuminate the day

I might be king awhile ...
                              but the blown spray
Is crimsoned in the sunset, and the wind
Blows coldly from the North ...

'The air indeed is chilly as you say.
Come in'.

'*Come in*'.
The company awaits us in the room.

In the second of *Three Poems*, 'Dead Season'—dedicated to Devlin—the poet seems to point a finger at his home-place and its lack, its denial:

What hope, though he stand in the porch at nightdown,
Stare down the slim grey road, what hopes turning
Twisting by us ...

Throughout these early poems written between "the fruiting and the early dream", the poet consistently returns either directly or metaphorically to the question of 'finding a place', a place for the imagination. This suggests, at the very least, a dissatisfaction with the traditional Irish interpretation that Coffey came up against at the time.

In his collection *Third Person* (1938), published in a series along with Samuel Beckett and Denis Devlin, this theme is recurrent—the contradictory pull of 'home', even while it stays hostile to him and the fate of his having to remain outside it. Here are two examples taken from the *Third Person.* In the first, notice the qualifying, almost dismissive "as they say":

I shall remember always as they say
a rock a lake a tree
birds and bread

while the following lines of final refusal come from 'Patience, No Memory':

Gather your flowers now
the house is ruined

the wind is free
beating wings long since
and white sails drive
anguish to anguish turned to stone

The elementary fusion of earth, fire and water that takes place in *Third Person* acts like forces which contain a spirit seeking metaphysical as much as real freedom. The almost complete exclusion in these early poems of a clearly discernible external world, as landscape or social scene, is important too because it is untypical of 20th-century Irish poetry. For the world 'out there' presents no real interest in the conventional sense for an imagination such as Brian Coffey's which wishes to purify, to render down experience to its essential moment of feeling or thoughtfulness. It is a poetry of self-awareness, pure and simple, steeped in the images of light which are so pervasive in the early collection. *Third Person* suggests, however, that, failing this possibility of freedom, there is only one way left, which is that taken in the collection's last poem 'One Way' and quoted here in full:

Giving what he has not given
he sees what he has not seen

Taking what he has not taken
he hears what he has not heard

No worst fear
no best light
constraint constrained
to work himself out

he breasts tide's breast

Again, we are presented with that impulse to journey in the concluding image, "he breasts tide's breast".

Having left Dublin in October 1937, and not to publish poetry until his return to England 20 years later from America, Brian Coffey spent the half-century in between on a remarkable voyage. With no definable audience and in a state of exile, his poetry became one major source of its own consolation: an inner dialogue. Time after time, in prose writings and in the occasional interview, Coffey has been emphatic about the necessary integrity of poetry and what he has called "the primordial aspect of the matter of art". And if his aloneness had been a costly one in personal terms, the poetry leads him out of his solitude. Indeed, the nature of his accomplishment as an artist acts as an exemplary contrast to much of what goes on in the business of poetry today. Coffey stands out by this very difference, the moral difference if you will, of his experience, and it gives an authority to what he writes, over and above the poetry's intrinsic value. It is an unusual authority because, while it is naturally dependent upon his work as a poet, it goes beyond the immediate and customary support and limitations of reputation, publicity and popularity that is so much associated with poetry now. This is not to suggest that Brian Coffey's isolation is an élitist thing. Far from it. Asked by Parkman Howe if he writes for any one group, for an Irish nation, or individuals, Coffey's reply perfectly illustrates the kind of contradictory relationship so relevant to this discussion of modern Irish poetry and its traditions:

> ... when I was in Paris I did start memorising French poems. But I didn't see the possibility of surviving in Paris, so that I didn't make the step, which would have involved two years in the army and naturalising myself as a citizen. When I came back here [England] into society the question was whether I was going to bother about an English audience at all. I had absolutely no desire to mix around London, meet anyone. I gradually came to see more and more that a person is at their best if they're on their home ground. I have always regretted that I haven't been able to remain in Ireland, because we could have had some fun. But since I haven't been able to end up in Ireland, the other thing I did was simply connect any work I did with Ireland, because that was nearer to the kind of things I felt instinctively. I think one is on safest ground, in poetry, when one is addressing what is human ... that strips away the nationalist quality.[6]

What Coffey has referred to as "the undertones of humility which induce a strength" emerge fairly clearly here. But, more importantly, there is the image of the poet which lies behind this quotation. For here too one senses a difference from the generally held view: on the one hand, a deliberate distance from the literary milieu—"no desire to mix around London, meet anyone"—and on the other hand, a clear-sighted commitment that "one is on safest ground, in poetry, when one is addressing what is human ... that strips away the nationalist quality".

Discussing Denis Devlin's "respect for all that effected the proper use of English", Coffey remarked in the *University Review*:

> I believe [Devlin] was quite unwilling to accept the idea of an Irish poet related parasitically or in some symbiosis of province or capital city to the London scene. Certainly not.[7]

Indeed, Devlin's poetry has this much in common with Coffey's, in that it overlooks 'the London scene' through an endeavour to absorb various different ideas and forms of European poetry into their own. As Victor Erlich states in his book *The Double Image*, what is at issue is not "the individual poet's view of himself as a human being but a more abstract ideational entity—notably the concept of the poet as an ideal type which informs the given artist's work and helps shape his life".[8] The image of the poet that both Coffey and Devlin (to a certain extent) share has led, in Devlin's case, to his being called 'obscure', most notably by that great name-caller, Randall Jarrell. Replying to such charges, Coffey maintained that

> ... the term obscurity, once used about a poet, has such a burr-like quality of sticking with bad effects on his reputation and on his sales, it is necessary to attempt to place such difficulty of meaning as does arise in Devlin's case in the correct perspective of his work as a whole.[9]

Coffey has effectively done this in his editing of Denis Devlin's poetry and through the various essays he has written on it. Devlin's mature work as a poet is never 'obscure' and the "difficulty of meaning" comes more from our expectations as readers than from any inherent perplexity in the writing.

For even a brief reading of Devlin's poetry reveals an attitude of poet to his world, and a general tone, that is mostly unheard of in modern Irish poetry.

> Evenings ever more willing lapse into my world's evening,
> Birds, like Imperial emblems, in their thin, abstract singing,
> Announce some lofty Majesty whose embassies are not understood,
> Thrushes' and finches' chords, like the yellow and blue skies changing
> place,
> I hold my stick, old-world, the waiters know me,
> And sip at my European drink, while sunlight falls,
> Like thick Italian silks over the square houses into the Bosphorus.

The poem, 'Memoirs of a Turcoman Diplomat', reveals the control which Denis Devlin exerts over his material. He is the poet of separation or, to use Coffey's effective phrase, Devlin is a poet of distance. He inhabits a territory in which few other Irish poets have been at home in their work. From his early experiments with surrealism in the 30s, to the forcefully structured *Lough Derg* poem (published in 1946) and *The Heavenly Foreigner* (republished in 1969 after its first appearance in 1950), Devlin's poetry has a fresh, worldly, masculine seriousness about it. There is little that is cramped, coy or clever about his poems. Some of them fail, particularly some of the early poems; but that, after all, is part and parcel of the risk of writing.

The poems he wrote in his student days and early adulthood are tuned to an operatic note of grand spectacular scenes and events: 'Before Lepanto: The Turkish Admiral Speaks to His Fleet' from *Poems* (1930); 'Entry of Multitudes into an Eternal Mansion', or 'Death and Her Beasts, Ignoble Beasts', from *Intercessions* (1937) and (originally published in the excellent but short-lived magazine, *Ireland Today*) with its macabre opening:

> The dried pus of vultures drags the horizon
> The noble beasts retired, their turn now, dried
> Mouths of my fears are death's vultures craving saliva:
> They would feed sick life on the smashed mouths of the weak
> Whose nostrils death has plugged with stale love-smells
> And suicide charms with racked face in a wall of marble,
> Their eyes decharged have numbness that looks like peace.

Devlin is a remote figure in the landscape of Irish poetry. Probably this is due to his rejection of much that has been conventionally understood to make up that landscape, both in his own day (barely 30 years ago) and ours. As he says in the 'Galway' section of 'The Heavenly Foreigner':

> it's no use turning aside, no use
> Staring through grey windows
> At the bent rain
> Slanting on grey seas

echoing, or perhaps rewriting, the concluding lines of a fine, previously unpublished, poem called 'Renewal by Her Element':

I knew the secret movements
Of the blood under your throat
And when we lay love-proven
Whispering legends to sleep
Braceleted in embrace
Your hands pouring on me
Fresh water of their caresses,
Breasts, nest of my tenderness,
All night was laced with praise.

Now my image faded
In the lucid fields
Of your eyes. Never again
Surprise for years, years.

My landscape is grey rain
Aslant on bent seas.

Devlin did not seek the comforts of tradition, but sought instead to extend it. His distance from the Irish literary world is testament to this fact. He cuts across our expectations; rebukes our complacent populism.

Devlin is a poet of passion in both the sensual and religious sense. His concerns as a poet are not caught up with, or bound by, any defining 'Irishness'. Nor is he reliant upon techniques and styles of writing that we usually associate with poetry in Ireland—portraits of landscape, nature; close imitation of speech and local turns of phrase; place-names. His American editors, themselves poets of distinction, Allen Tate and Robert Penn Warren, have written in their introduction to a selection of Devlin's poetry:

> ... there are almost no traces of Yeats' 'romantic Ireland' of the Celtic Twilight. Devlin was one of the international poetic English which now [1963] prevails on both sides of the Atlantic.

Indeed, on this question of Devlin's use of language, his pioneering of an 'international poetic English' distinct from traditional Irish forms, it is interesting to note what the Irish novelist John Banville has written:

> Listen to any group of Irish people conversing, from whatever class, in

> whatever circumstances, and behind the humour and the rhetoric and the slyness you will detect a dark note of hopelessness before the phenomenon of a world that is always out there. [10]

It was as if Devlin had to find a new kind of language in order to penetrate the traditional poetic barriers to the "phenomenon of a world that is always out there" and, in so doing, stepped beyond the conventions. His poetry also can be read from the viewpoint that he sought, through it, to overcome the dark note, of which Banville speaks, in an effort to move into the world. This was a necessary condition for his writing; the starting point of his poetry.

Indeed, the chief quality that comes across from Devlin's poetry is its formal strength and reserve, the poet's unindulgent acceptance of being a poet and getting on with it, negotiating the poetry through his own life and experience of the world he lives in, rather than some idealised vision or literary version of it. This is the first part of 'Little Elegy', for instance, which recounts his time in Munich (1931), written soon afterwards and published in *Ireland Today*:

> I will walk with a lover of wisdom
> A smile for Senator Destiny
> But I shall gladly listen.
>
> Her beauty was like silence in a cup of water
> Decanting all but the dream matter
> The figures of reality
> Stood about, Dantesque and pitiful.
> Can anyone tell me her name?
> I will love her again and again
> Girl on skis, arrow and bow in one,
> Masked in glass, graceful,
> Hard as a word in season.
>
> I saw a round, Bavarian goodman
> And a Harvard student with a Mohican's lope
> Colliding with huge nosegays
> Then laughter burst above their flowers:
> Absent of mind, they had their wits about them
> I laughed at them both outright
>
> And at simpering, peasant statues
> Graces and gods would they be!

It was a heady springtime in Munich
Many I knew confided in me
Popu, the champion cyclist
Sigmund, deriding tyrants
And Carlos, who made love shyly
To a furtive, gentle girl
And came to my door, stammering,
'She loves me, you know.'
'She loves me, you know.'
But geography separated them
And geography keeps them apart
Now they live forgotten in each other's heart.

In 'After Five O'Clock', the poet sees how complex illusions are between a professional bureaucrat and the locals, who, by chance, are left together in a tavern:

A Government official dressed in grey minor
Slipped into a low pub
At the end of the world;
Outside, the rain was falling in millions.

An ancient like a frittered, chalk hill
Monocled the evening paper through a chip of window-pane:
The disgraced words took on dignity.

'Will he tout me for a drink?' feared the Government official
Though the ancient stirred no more than a thought in a new-dead man.

Behind these contingencies (and behind the lines from the previous poem "geography separated them/And geography keeps them apart") is Devlin's experience of otherness, strangeness, the fact of not being in one's own place, the fact of realising that there is no place that is 'one's own': we make it so; need it to be so. It is an illusion. Separation exposes this truth: it is the exile's condition, since he is basically kept apart by his past life and by who he is: "a generic feature of the artist's rootless plight" as much as "a specifically Irish form of alienation", to conjoin the terms of Seamus Deane's comment. Denis Devlin's poems throw us back upon these unsettling conclusions.

Indeed, Devlin is reported as saying that the only good thing about the diplomatic corps, of which he was a prominent member from the late 30s to the time of his death in 1959, was that it got you out of

Ireland. In common with other poets like the Greek Seferis, Chile's Neruda, the Polish Milosz and Saint John Perse, the French poet he translated, Devlin's experience of life as a diplomat underlines his sense of himself as a poet. His poems, for instance, are often set in exotic climates and unusual settings, yet running through them is a perpetual sense of distance, of not being fixed in one's native place but feeling free of it.

One of his most powerful poems, 'From Government Buildings', relates this feeling of the poet as a separate figure, monitoring moments that show history-in-prism; as one man's life in reasoned proportion to his own time:

> Evening lapses. No pity or pain, the badgered
> Great get home, and the little, tomorrow's anchorage,
> All smiling, sour the milk of charity,
> Like the pyrrhonist poets, Love's saboteurs.
>
> The clerks fan out and the lamps; and I look inwards:
> What turns amuse you now? with whom, not me! do
> You cower in Time, whose palsied pulse is nimbler
> A hair's breadth when want and have are equal?
>
> My room sighs empty with malignant waiting;
> The November wind slows down outside, wheeling
> Twig and awning on the brick balcony,
> A wind with hackles up. In Rome at evening
>
> Swallows traced eggshapes on the vellum sky,
> The wind was warm with blue rain in Dublin;
> When the culture-heroes explored the nether world
> It was voiceless beasts on the move made Death terrible.

The sense here of city-life, of the clerks and lamps spreading out into a Dantesque vision, is dramatised further in Thomas Kinsella's major poem, 'Nightwalker'. While the "culture-heroes" in Devlin's 'From Government Buildings' have taken on a more specific shape in Kinsella's, the vision in both poems returns to 'the self' and its awkward, unstable relation to the world:

> I must lie down with them all soon and sleep,
> And rise with them again when the new dawn
> Has touched our pillows and our wet pallor

And roused us. We'll come scratching in our waistcoats
Down to the kitchen for a cup of tea;
Then with our briefcases, through wind or rain,
Past our neighbours' gardens—Melrose, Bloomfield—
To wait at the station, fluttering our papers,
Palping the cool wind, discussing and murmuring.[11]

'Nightwalker' contains many of the stresses I have been discussing so far. As a poem which is conscious of the place within it of the poet himself, 'Nightwalker' also seeks to find, or make an alignment with, some new configuration of tradition. The exhortations to Joyce, for instance, as

Watcher in the tower, be with me now
At your parapet, above the glare of the lamps.
Turn your milky spectacles on the sea
Unblinking; cock your ear [12]

and to Swift, "Father of Authors!", shows Kinsella trying to regroup the relevant artistic powers so that they may confront, through his poem, an impoverished and impoverishing contemporary world. It is a struggle with which Kinsella's poetry generally contends, indicting the past and exploring its myth-like proportions in his own life. The old and dark woman's shape "like a hunting bird's" in 'Ancestor', for example, has the predatory omniscience that engulfs the poem's narrator, brushing him aside, so to speak, with a terrible self-preoccupation:

I was going up to say something,
and stopped. Her profile against the curtains
was old, and dark like a hunting bird's.

It was the way she perched on the high stool,
staring into herself, with one fist
gripping the side of the barrier around her desk
—or her head held by something, from inside.
And not caring for anything around her
or anyone there by the shelves.
I caught a faint smell, musky and queer.

I may have made some sound—she stopped rocking
and pressed her fist in her lap; then she stood up

and shut down the lid of the desk, and turned the key.
She shoved a small bottle under her aprons
and came toward me, darkening the passageway.

Ancestor ... among sweet- and fruit-boxes
Her black heart ...
                    Was that a sigh?
—brushing by me in the shadows,
with her heaped aprons, through the red hangings
to the scullery, and down to the back room.

It is as if the world which the 'Ancestor' embodies is an alien one, even to an onlooker so familiar with it. This gap of dislocation recurs throughout Kinsella's poetry. It is the crucial perceptual space between him and the subjects of his poetry which forces us, in turn, to reconsider our relation to them. Underlying this disturbance, there is, too, the persistent question of where the poet and poem stand in relation to what has gone before, to what Kinsella has called the "turning confidently toward an act of self-scrutiny and redefinition".

In 'Poetry since Yeats: An Exchange of Views', Kinsella refers to the poet's isolation in Ireland:

> Up to 1955 or so the feeling is one of isolation—isolation from war and then from dynamic post-war phenomena in literature, economics and everything else: an Ireland hardly aware of what modern men and nations were demanding of themselves. The poets and writers who liked to call themselves Literary Dublin survived Yeats in a closed world, writing Georgian verses for each other, but giving it a 'sweet wild Gaelic twist'.[13]

While acknowledging that since "1955 or so there have been some changes, on the whole for the better", Kinsella emphatically returns to this point of dislocation and of how pervasive the condition is:

> After the deluge, the Poet is still naturally isolated, but so now is everyman ... the most sensitive individuals have been shaken loose into disorder, conscious of a numbness and dullness in themselves, a pain of dislocation and loss.

Nothing can be taken for granted. As Kinsella writes, "for the present it seems that every writer has to make the imaginative grasp at identity for himself".[14] It is a feeling that Kinsella conveys in many of his poems, of 'dislocation and loss', as in 'A Country Walk', significantly *without* looking for easy resolutions in false nostalgia or forced bravado.

Kinsella's poetry is full of journeys, both outwards around a known terrain or within, towards, an unknown world. He sees, for instance in 'A Country Walk' or in 'Ritual of Departure', the interstices of past and present as they glut into a tenuous and contradictory pull between the continuity of tradition and the disruption of the present:

> Stones of a century and a half ago.
> The same city distinct in the same air,
> More open in an earlier evening light.
> Dublin under the Georges ...
> stripped of Parliament,
> Lying powerless in sweet-breathing death-ease
> after forced Union.
> Under a theatre of swift-moving cloud
> Domes, pillared, in the afterglow—
> A portico, beggars moving on the steps—
>
> A horserider locked in soundless greeting,
> Bowed among dogs and dung; the panelled vista
> Closing on pleasant smoke-blue far-off hills.
>
> *
>
> The ground opens. Pale wet potatoes
> Break into light. The black soil falls from their flesh,
> From the hands that tear them up and spread them out
> In fresh disorder, perishable roots to eat.
> ...
> I scoop at the earth, and sense famine, a first
> Sourness in the clay. The roots tear softly.

The roots that "tear softly" are those fragile membranes that poetry can restore to a life. Kinsella has explored this theme in other terms as well when he states, in 'The Irish Writer', that

> ... if the function of tradition is to link us living with the significant past, this is done as well by a broken tradition as by a whole one—however painful it may be humanly speaking. I am certain that a great part of the significance of my own past, as I try to write my poetry, is that that past *is* mutilated.[15]

The imagination thus becomes a medium through which that mutilated past is both recorded and also healed. Poetry is redemptive. On the one hand, a poem stands in a questioning and questionable relationship to the present and, on the other, the poet gathers into the poem whatever significance he can from the drifting past.

It is important to note at this stage how Kinsella places such responsibility upon the individual poet when, in his contribution to the symposium on 'Poetry since Yeats', he remarked that since it is "out of ourselves and our wills that the chaos came ... out of ourselves ... some order will have to be constructed". The emphasis falls upon Kinsella's use of the word *constructed,* in keeping with the weight he gives to the notion of the poet as an artist who consciously works and shapes his or her writing.

In his 1962 interview with Peter Orr, published in *The Poet Speaks,* Kinsella remarks: "Of poets those I respect most are the formal constructors of poems" and he singles out "the conscious, constructed fabrication of the human intellect and spirit like Dante and Keats, and the later Yeats." Similarly, in his poem 'Magnanimity', dedicated to Austin Clarke and set in Coole Park, Kinsella sees the poetic imagination leading a houseless, fugitive existence:

> I am sure that there are no places for poets,
> Only changing habitations for verse to outlast.

There are, in other words, few traditional consolations for the poet in this day and age, except for those which are discovered by himself. The poet must literally make himself; this is the inescapable experience of *being* a poet in the world today.

Talking of this fundamental condition in 'The Irish Writer', Kinsella is adamant:

> Relationship to tradition, whether broken or not, is only part of the story. For any writer there is also the relationship with other literatures, with the present, with the 'human predicament', with the self. This last may be the most important of all, for certain gaps in ourselves can swallow up all the potentiality in the world.[16]

There may have been in Ireland too much preoccupation with 'tradition' (and with establishing the individual poet's relationship to it) as a way of validating received codes and beliefs. This critical perspective needs to be balanced with the differences that exist between Irish poets through those terms of reference to which Kinsella refers—"other literatures, with the present, with the 'human predicament', with the self."

The work of the three poets I have looked briefly at here necessitates such a shift of emphasis before it can be properly understood. Yet if we have come to accept certain customary ways of reading Irish poetry, these clichés will always run the risk of being taken for granted and accepted as the whole truth. This points to the kind of literary tradition and society in which the poet lives and writes in Ireland. Yet only when a poet has actually separated his/herself from the past and his/her heritage, and has imaginatively transcended it, can he or she become truly effective, truly him or herself. The process goes against the grain. The Irish seek to maintain, at the very least, an illusion of being forever of the one place and of the one people through an eternal affair with 'the Irish tradition'. Seemingly, to cut across this inherited bond is taken as some kind of betrayal.

Unlike, for instance, Patrick Kavanagh, who has had such a major, indeed predominant, influence upon Irish poetry, the position of the three poets I have been discussing is significantly different. For their example has not been generally assessed and absorbed into the creative and critical wellspring of Irish poetry or made sufficiently available to us as options. Failure to do this promotes an orthodox view which, while it might comfort us, does not encourage the kind of imaginative exploration, confidence and freedom that we all seek to find and secure in every work of art.

Notes

Unless otherwise stated, the poetry quoted in this essay is taken from the following texts: Brian Coffey, *Selected Poems* (Dublin: New Writers' Press, 1971); *The Complete Poems of Denis Devlin*, edited by Brian Coffey, (Dublin, 1964); Thomas Kinsella, *Poems, 1956-1973* (Mountrath: Dolmen Press, 1980). Some of the material included in this essay is drawn from a series of radio talks produced by Cathal O'Griofa and presented by the author on RTE in 1985.

[1] Seamus Deane, *Celtic Revivals* (London: Faber and Faber, 1985) p. 156.

[2] James Mays, Introductory Essay to *Irish University Review*, 5, no. 1 (Spring 1975), p.12.

[3] Stan Smith, 'On Other Grounds: The Poetry of Brian Coffey', in *Two Decades of Irish Writing*, edited by Douglas Dunn (Cheadle Hulme, Cheshire: Carcanet Press, 1975), p. 59.

[4] Coffey, *Selected Poems*, p. 29.

[5] First published in *Criterion*, 18, no. 70, (1938), pp. 37-38.

[6] *Eire/Ireland*, 13, no. 1 (Spring 1978), p. 122.

[7] *University Review*, 2, no. 11 (1961), p. 12.

[8] Victor Erlich, *The Double Image* (Baltimore, 1964), p. 1.

[9] *Poetry Ireland*, 2 (1963), p. 79.

[10] *Irish University Review*, 11 (Spring 1981), p. 14.

[11] Kinsella, *Poems, 1956-73*, pp. 103-4.

[12] ibid., p. 108.

[13] *Tri-Quarterly*, no. 4 (196) p. 106.

[14] Thomas Kinsella, *Davis, Mangan, Ferguson? Tradition and the Irish Writer* (Dublin: Dolmen Press 1970) p. 66.

[15] ibid., p. 66.

[16] ibid., p. 65.

4

Heroic Heart

Charles Donnelly

I

In an article called 'A Memory of Charles Donnelly', published in the English literary magazine, *Iron* (October/December1980), Ewart Milne had this to say about his young friend killed during the battle of Jarama on 27th February, 1937, aged 22:

> Charles Donnelly has been sadly neglected as a poet, both in Ireland and over here in England. And not simply because he left so few poems. He suffered the fate of all Irish poets of the 30s, that of being ignored, neglected.

Milne has also referred to the Irish poets of the 30s as "a lost generation", eclipsed in a sense, initially, by the dominating contemporary presence of W.B. Yeats and, subsequently, scattered by World War II.

While that generation was never a clearly defined 'group', the 30s in Ireland present the literary critic and social historian with a definable cultural context within which 'Charlie' Donnelly can be placed, along with the general beliefs he held in common with other writers of the time. These beliefs were both social and literary in nature. The radical reassessment of what had and what had not been achieved in Ireland since the Rising of 1916, through the bloody conflict of the Civil War, towards the establishment of de Valera's Constitution, were part and parcel of the cultural climate.

The doubts, disillusionment, emotional complication and plans of the time, with Ireland on the verge of independence, made it all the more difficult for the artist to understand what his or her relationship was to be with the fledgling state. This was exacerbated by the official ruling attitudes to 'culture', which were consummated in the Censorship Act of 1929 and which set the tone for the following two decades and more.

It was, effectively, an institutionalisation of one version of Irish life and literature, heavily dependent upon the inherited Victorian idea of tradition as a legacy of moral truths and domestic virtues.

As C.M. Bowra remarked in *Poetry and Politics: 1900-1960* (1966), dealing with another period of cultural consolidation:

> Bourgeois [the] word has been worked to death, and the only point of reviving it is to show that in their years of repression the Russians encouraged a poetry which was indeed bourgeois in the most pejorative sense—unadventurous, conventional, sentimental, and uninspired.

While the repression in Ireland cannot be compared on any level to the scale of savagery enacted by Stalin's purges, Bowra's comment about the bourgeois nature of the official culture has direct relevance to the Ireland against which Charles Donnelly defined himself as poet and republican activist. Yet it would be presumptuous to suggest that this negative motivation was his sole inspiration.

Ewart Milne met Donnelly in London and it is significant that both poets were outside Ireland from at least 1936 onwards—an indication that the conservative *mores* and beliefs had triumphed in Ireland. Donnelly and Milne, and the many other contributors to the left-wing magazine, *Ireland Today*, for instance, represent a rearguard action against the encroaching stultification of the literary scene in Ireland, a situation that was to be consolidated throughout the euphemistically-entitled 'Emergency' (World War II) and well into the 50s, claiming as its victims such brilliant minds as Flann O'Brien (a contemporary of Donnelly's at University College, Dublin), Patrick Kavanagh and, later, Brendan Behan.

The positive response to this situation is to be found in the literature which set out to challenge that "unadventurous, conventional, sentimental, and uninspired" writing which was regularly published and held up as the true reflection of Irish life. It was a reflection de Valera sought to fix in the minds of his public when, in 1933, he broadcast the following words:

> You sometimes hear Ireland charged with a narrow and intolerant nationalism, but Ireland today has no dearer hope than this: that, true to her holiest traditions, she should humbly serve the truth, and help by truth to save the world.

Not exactly the kind of sentiment which Donnelly or Milne could whole-heartedly endorse, given the fact, as Milne records, that "we were both a bit outside our respective Churches". De Valera went on to spell out soberly the ideals of this austerely disciplined vision:

> Ireland united, Ireland free, Ireland self-supporting, and self-reliant, Ireland speaking her own tongue and through it giving to the world the ancient treasures of Christian Gaelic culture.

Looking back, it seems inevitable that this vision was bound to frustrate the imaginative and political explorations that a poet such as Charles Donnelly was making. There is, consequently, something peculiarly poignant about the image Ewart Milne creates of the young Donnelly, exiled from home and the struggles of Dublin, entering the offices of the Spanish Medical Aid Committee in the late autumn of 1936:

> His was a slight figure, with a large thoughtful head, and large intensely blue eyes. He told us he was looking for something to do, preferably for Spain, for a while, until he was called up into the International Brigade.

From this point in 1936 to early the next year, it seems that Donnelly was actively contributing to various left-wing newspapers, giving lectures, writing poetry and meeting Milne:

> We gradually drew together, through talking 'Dublin-shop' and soon were walking what Paddy Kavanagh called the 'savage streets of London' by night, drinking endless cups of coffee at Joe Lyons Tea Shops, with an occasional roll if we were flush.

Shortly afterwards, Donnelly left for the Spanish Civil War and, in one of the most important early engagements of the International Brigade, the battle of Jarama, Donnelly, to quote from *The Book of the XVth Brigade* (Madrid 1938) "fell charging the Fascist trenches ... his body, shattered by two explosive bullets, was recovered four days later".

The short span of Donnelly's life conceals both the tension and intensity of these eager commitments and aspirations. It would be impractical in the space available to detail the places and times of his life, from those whom he knew during his Tyrone childhood, in Dundalk, to his years as an undergraduate at University College, Dublin; his political beliefs that brought him in contact with the socialist republican movement in Dublin, to his months in London before joining the International Brigade, and his subsequent political career leading towards the fight against the Fascists in Spain.

It would also be insensitive to the fierce balance of Donnelly's life if one were to overstate the drift, political as much as personal, that led him, like so many of his English and a number of his Irish contemporaries, to Spain. As with other members of the International Brigade, there was in the urgent demands of war-torn Spain, a necessary readjustment of theory to experience, an adjustment we have little means at present to document, except to say that it was foreshadowed in Donnelly's own poetry. The significance of Spain can, however, become exaggerated, the literary work of the period engulfed by its political realities and given a value it does not, as literature, possess. Conversely, the conventional notions of poetry in Ireland are peculiarly exclusive, in that figures such as Charles Donnelly have not been sufficiently read and critically evaluated. Possibly this is because of the political connotations of the period or because of the challenge such work presents to our customary modes of thinking about Irish poetry.

II

Samuel Hynes, in his classic study *The Auden Generation* (1979), has shown how that generation grew to define itself within two terms: the Great War of 1914-18 and its apprehension of World War II. The mixture of guilt at not having fought in the Great War, of an abstract, anti-militarism, and the sense of absence, of being a 'buffer-generation', were features of the Auden generation. The level of coherence here is a result of hindsight, but, as Hynes charts, the well-known poets of the 30s had experiences in common which generated an atmosphere of self-consciousness and of cultural homogeneity. What happened to the generation after the hammer-blows of events such as the Spanish Civil War is another matter, but the 30s' poets in

England make a useful comparison with the Irish situation.

The Irish political gears were in a different order: violence was not an imagined thing nor civil war a premonition; Ireland had experienced a savage and retributive war, small in scale but grievously intense. It had narrowed into a distorted perspective the demands of the Easter Rising and created a dialectic of disillusionment and retrenched hope. The alternative was exile, voluntary or otherwise.

Charles Donnelly's poetry moves in a similar pattern, and like his slightly older contemporaries and many of his peers, he was profoundly influenced by the lack, in Ireland, of a cultural atmosphere that was *relevant* to modern life and literature.

This was summarised most forcibly by Samuel Beckett when, writing as 'Andrew Belis', he stated that "the breakdown of the object, whether current, historical, mythical or spook" was the "rupture of the lines of communication". To be unaware of this was to remain an antiquarian hack. This fragmentation, echoing the social life of Ireland during the late 20s and early 30s, expressed itself imaginatively as an endeavour, then and subsequently, for poets to write, not in the rhetorical fashion of Yeats, but rather in the manner of Joyce. Ironically, perhaps, Donnelly wrote a defence of Yeats against the charge of being 'non-national' in University College, Dublin's student magazine, *Comthrom Feinne* (April 1932), proclaiming, in Joycean style, that the "artist expresses his own soul, not that of a nation nor of a mob".

Donnelly's precocious proclamation was defiant, but it is not absorbed in his early poems. They are love poems addressed in abstract ways to a someone, or something lost, leaving the poet dreaming, vulnerable, his thoughts 'borne away' in Shelleyan wonder. Yet 'In a Library' (January 1933) anticipates the tone of the later mature poems:

> Are the moods voiceless? For I have no words.
> Blood cannot talk, although it cracked the skin.

The sense here of the tense relatedness of mind, thought and the physical, is the dominant note in Donnelly's poetry. In the same year as 'In a Library' was published, he wrote again in *Comthrom Feinne*: "Antagonism to thought actually precedes setting off thought against experience. But there is no opposition. Thought does not occur in a void." In his poetry, and elsewhere, Donnelly tries to draw thought and experience into an ever closer relationship. He sets them in metaphorical harmony without idealising that harmony in pathetic fictions. The poems are worked by uncompromising verbs into terse and stark declarations, such as in this extract from 'Approach' (April, 1934):

> The tightening eyes, tendrilled of sympathy,
> The accepted secret before a third;
> The unrequired gesture, imperfect denial of contact.

The poem is tautly worked and deals with the strange secretive signs of a meeting between lovers, observed by another. The "tightening eyes, tendrilled of sympathy" are relaxed, after the gestures, by "sudden tenderness lightening in simple actions", finally confirmed in "mutual and offered laughter". The psychological perceptiveness of 'Approach' is found in other poems, such as 'Wages of Deviation' and 'Unnoticed in Hurry of Callous Good-bye'. Poems of this order have a conclusive, driving syntax which could appear relentless were it not for Donnelly's dramatic gift, as seen in his 1934 poem, 'The Flowering Bars':

> After sharp words from the fine mind,
> protest in court,
> the intimate high head constrained,
> strait lines of prison, empty walls,
> a subtle beauty in a simple place.
>
> There to strain thought through the tightened brain,
> there weave
> the slender cords of thought, in calm,
> until routine in prospect bound
> joy into security,
> and among strictness sweetness grew,
> mystery of flowering bars.

The rhetorical resonance (remembering Donnelly's admiration for Yeats) of the first three lines of 'The Flowering Bars', the factual fourth line subduing the mannerism of "protest in court" strikes an imaginative resolution with "a subtle beauty in a simple place". The poem proceeds, by way of the pivotal tension in thought ("through the tightened brain"), to an elaboration of the statement ("a subtle beauty in a simple place"). The dialectic of routine/prospect, joy/ security, strictness/sweetness is consolidated in the expressive ambiguity of "mystery of flowering bars", giving the poem a self-inclusive strength.

The same form is at work in 'Unnoticed in Hurry of Callous Good-bye' (1934) and particularly in 'Wages of Deviation' (1934) where "youth's lonely, austere joy" is broken by physical contact, "bringing elation, opening/through the white summer roads, the world". The resolution here, is transitory, describing how "Through love's complications", "touch acquired the delicacy of speech/and speech invaded apprehending flesh". In the aftermath of 'resentment', there is a 'truce':

> ... your memory,
> hair blown fine against lamplight, makes
> my heart and hands go wild.

The poem is an acknowledgement of conflict, its persistence, and of how the poet deals with both through a distancing of experience that neither idealises nor obscures the love that is lost.

During 1935, Donnelly concentrated on polemical reading and active politics and wrote little poetry. In London later that year, and throughout 1936, his name appeared over several articles in left-wing publications, such as the Communist Party's *International Press Correspondence*, the *Left Review* and the *Irish Front.*

III

In 'The Tolerance of Crows', however, which Donnelly had shown Ewart Milne "about the end of 1936, or into 1937", the poet counter-poses Death with its own impersonality—an objective meditation remote from the sentimentalised versions of martyrdom and sacrifice that were so common in Ireland barely two decades earlier:

> Death comes in quantity from solved
> Problems on maps, well-ordered dispositions,
> Angles of elevation and direction;
>
> Comes innocent from tools children might

Love, retaining under pillows,
Innocently impales on any flesh.

And with flesh falls apart the mind
That trails thought from the mind that cuts
Thought clearly for a waiting purpose.

Progress of poison in the nerves and
Discipline's collapse is halted.
Body awaits the tolerance of crows.

Without despair or burdensome self-consciousness, Donnelly's poem is unnerving: the shifts of perception sound the poem's emotional depths. From "maps" and "well-ordered dispositions" to the "tools" of guns children might innocently retain, the meaning of death, framed by the "options" of cowardice or breakdown, is stated with the poet's full imaginative control. Donnelly's poetry is impressive because of this balance, achieved through the exact measure of the lines themselves: "Death", he writes,

Comes innocent from tools children might
Love, retaining under pillows,
Innocently impales on any flesh.

The movement of the line is cumulative, offering alternatives along the way, almost misleading us: death's equivalents are "in quantity", "dispositions"; it is something a child might love by proxy of the tools, until we are forced into the blunt contradiction of "Innocently *impales* on *any* flesh" revealing the true nature of wartime death. In making this kind of restrained personification, Donnelly does not obliterate the source of the poem: the self waiting for death. The poem's achievement is that there is nothing passive in the waiting, the mind in *engaged*, thinking; it is an experience, so to speak, of death's imminence.

'Heroic Heart' extends this theme, but its idiom is less incisive and compressed. The poem, in comparison, is expansive, moving out from the blunt centre to take in other perspectives, psychological and physical:

And cry music under a storm of 'planes,
Making thrust head to slacken, muscle waver
And intent mouth recall old tender tricks.

In such circumstances, "only leafless plants/And earth retain disinterestedness". The accord of mind and body, instantly united under attack, is almost animalistic; an instinctive understanding:

> Thought, magnetised to lie of the land, moves
> Heartily over the map wrapped in its iron
> Storm. Battering the roads, armoured columns
> Break walls of stone or bone without receipt.
> Jawbones find new ways with meat, loins
> Raking and blind, new ways with women.

Donnelly's political or philosophical beliefs manifest themselves in his poetry in a passage such as this. He thought of himself as a Marxist, and 'Heroic Heart' reveals the conflicting claims of self and world rendered compatible, if still in tension, by the imagery of action. It is Donnelly's *style* which embodies his Marxism. (By 'style' I mean that crucial expression of one's own ideas, the form of the voice, the stress of syntax, the mobility of line, the range of metaphor and symbol.) Generally speaking, Donnelly's poems maintain a balance between the impact of experience and the adequacy of language to deal with it. One reading of his poetry could propose that, while aware of what Beckett believed to be the disruption of communication, with the lines between self and world, subject and object, broken down, Donnelly attempted to preserve discourse, and that this attempt was rooted in his Marxism. His poems strain under this awareness. Yet he writes without recourse to a supportive system of mythological, literary or topographical reference, in contrast to contemporaries such as Brian Coffey or Denis Devlin. Donnelly's poetry, as a result, is all the more dependent within itself for imaginative scope and elucidation and upon the critical intelligence and aggressive syntax at work. This reveals the perplexed union of thought and feeling, deed and idea: "*tightened* brain", "*tightening* eyes", "purpose *crossed*", "*contracted* heart", "head *constrained*", "Thought, *magnetised*", "thought's *invasion*", and so on (my italics).

In 'Poem', Donnelly writes explicitly about the forces which converge upon the mind of the poet. It is a poem about balance and is itself remarkably proportioned. In the characteristic distancing of 'self' in his poems, 'Poem' reads as a soliloquy, with Donnelly relinquishing the past, the "private study and the public/Defiance". What remains is "simple action only on which will flickers/Catlike".

All else, "Name, subject of all-considered words, praise and blame", is "Irrelevant". The self is either obliterated in death or "strait confinement" or the occasion for "orators,/Figure stone-struck beneath damp Dublin sky". Yet Donnelly, having followed again the options that are before him, reveals that hidden away from the aldermen who cheer, teachers who make oblique references in class and the mystifying "gum of sentiment" spun around erroneously accredited "qualities", there is the unassailable self:

> The technique of the public man, the masked servilities are
> Not for you. Master of military trade, you give
> Like Raleigh, Lawrence, Childers, your services but not yourself.

It is a rare occasion, as Donnelly imparts 'outside' information about himself: an ethic of will that Hemingway would applaud? A wry joke at his own expense? Or an answer to the exigencies of his time? Donnelly's poetry is a technique worked out for survival.

IV

The poems 'Tolerance of Crows', 'Heroic Heart' and 'Poem' were published in *Ireland Today*, apparently through the good offices of Donagh Mac Donagh, a college contemporary of Donnelly. The magazine's biographical notes on contributors describes Donnelly as a "revolutionary poet in matter and manner of whom we shall hear more in this and other fields". He was dead the following month, and the magazine was to close within a year's time.

As Terence Brown has remarked in *Ireland: A Social and Cultural History 1922-1985* (1985):

> *Ireland Today* gave a platform to some of these writers and to intellectuals whose concerns were European as well as Irish. The journal was one of the very few places in Ireland where support for the republican cause in Spain had any overt expression.

It is, therefore, no accident that Milne and Donnelly were contributors, but it would be an oversimplification for us to see *Ireland Today*, and indeed the relationship between Milne and his younger contemporary, Donnelly, solely in terms of the Spanish Civil War. Their contributions to *Ireland Today*, for instance, were literary, and neither poet contributed anything of an overtly political nature, although one could say that Milne's stories come close to such a description.

Their relationship seems to have been based, so far as one can ever define such things, upon similar experiences and creative needs, even while their backgrounds were dissimilar.

As Milne describes their vigil walks through London, both figures seem like emigrés "discussing the springs of poetry, our own poems".

> We did 'swop' poems, however, I mean we showed each other what we were writing at that time, and ... I can well remember my interest in 'The Flowering Bars' which [Donnelly] told me he had written in Dublin, before he left.

This sense of exile emerges too from Donnelly's writing of the period, in, for instance, his 'Portrait of a Revolution', written for the *Left Review* (October 1935), where he describes a German refugee:

> ... in that month-old English, so bare that it required eking out with physical gestures, one became acquainted with a mind which three years of underground fighting had so matured that against its realism the clever, eager voices in the room sounded blatantly young and far-fetched. It did not take long to discover that there was not a grain of sentimentality, posturing or illusion left to obscure the vision of this man. He was perfectly in touch with life.

And, of course, this was a period when to be "perfectly in touch with life" was synonymous with political action. It also meant the responsibility to expose "sentimentality, posturing or illusion", a responsibility that implicated the writer and both Milne's and Donnelly's poetry of the time accepted this demand. It appears, though, that this clear-sightedness underwent a profound change during the actual experience of the Spanish Civil War. In his 'A Memory', Ewart Milne is explicit on this point:

> I have considered this very carefully, but I think I can say that I fully intended to follow Charlie into the [International] Brigade, to link up with him. But somehow, when I was told of his death, I turned away, and gradually, though I continued bringing out supplies ... I turned away also from the whole scene.

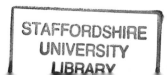

A similar 'turning away' seems to have taken place with Donnelly if we accept the testimony of his friend Donagh MacDonagh, who has written in 'Club Sans Club' (*University Review*, 1958):

> [Donnelly] was made a Military Commissar, a post of great danger, and before his death ... he had lost sympathy with his comrades, or so I deduced from a cryptic post-card which he sent to me a few weeks before. 'Tell A.B. I would now agree with him', he wrote. A.B. was anti-communist.

Another failed God? It is difficult to ascertain Donnelly's feelings during the last weeks of his life. Few of his personal letters and other related manuscripts have been located. What is clear, though, is the importance of that precarious relationship struck between the two poets, Milne and Donnelly, in the latter half of 1936 and early 1937. As Milne remembers:

> ... I did not want to fight any more. But I did mourn for Charlie Donnelly, oh, not in the usual sense, not even for the fine poet he was, but simply, for my little friend.

Donnelly, anticipating his own fate, wrote in 'Poem', which had been postered on the battalion's mural wall:

> Your flag is public over granite. Gulls fly above it.
> Whatever the issue of the battle is, your memory
> Is public, for them to pull awry with crooked hands,
> Moist eyes. And village reputations will be built on
> Inaccurate accounts of your campaign. You're name for orators,
> Figure stone-struck beneath damp Dublin sky.

In repudiating the vain memorialists, the "gum of sentiment ... qualities attributed in error", "the public talk which sounds the same on hollow/Tongue as true", Donnelly entered the imaginations of those who, grieving his loss, saw the young poet as a symbol of something he had achieved beyond himself—as in Blanaid Salkeld's 'Casualties', Donagh Mac Donagh's 'He is Dead and Gone, Lady' and, more recently, in Michael Longley's fine elegy 'Even the Olives Are Bleeding'.

In Ewart Milne's dedicatory poem, we have more starkly revealed what that loss meant. "It was really a shock to me. I had really liked the little poet, and I grieved for him, and it was out of that I wrote the poem, 'Thinking of Artolas'."

Sirs and Senoras, let me end my story—
I show you earth, earth formally,
And Two on guard with the junipers.
Two, Gael and Jew side by side in a trench
Gripping antique guns to flick at the grasshoppers
That zoomed overhead and the moon was rocking.
Two who came from prisonment, Gael because of Tone,
Jew because of human love, the same for Jew as German—
Frail fragments both, chipped off and forgotten readily ...

I set them together, Izzy Rupchik and Donnelly;
And of that date with death among the junipers
I say only, they kept it ...

V

There are few enough poems upon which Charles Donnelly's reputation as a poet rests. Yet his short life is full of an overshadowing expectation that seems to eclipse his actual poetic accomplishment. If Donnelly was, according to Eavan Boland, a dark star, perhaps we have been unclear about the nature of its light.

In a way, this is to be expected. The Irish poets of the 30s, Donnelly, Devlin, Coffey and others, have still not received anything like the critical attention they deserve. It is easier to leap from the 30s by concentrating upon those magnificent lyrics of Yeats; from there, the shape of Irish poetry is really a foregone conclusion. But the poets who started out in the early 30s went on to probe and explore many different avenues, their language and styles challenging what was conventional and orthodox in the poetry of the time, and indeed to the present.

As a result of this neglect, our reading of modern Irish poetry remains flawed, while our knowledge of the lives behind that poetry is anecdotal. Joseph Donnelly's *Memoir* (1987) exposes the inadequacies of our literary history. For in that book Charles's brother begins a new story, one that we have not heard before. It is of middle-class Catholic Ireland, first based in Tyrone, from there to Dundalk, and eventually Dublin.

It is of a prosperous, industrious family, through whose eyes we see the intense and questing young Charlie becoming estranged as a result of his political commitments with republican and socialist organisations, first in University College, Dublin, and, later, outside college. We have a sense of the sheer weight of Dublin bourgeois conservatism, but also of the intense family bonds that were so deeply a part of Donnelly's own make-up.

There is the love-affair with Cora Hughes, de Valera's goddaughter, the whirlwind of meetings and debates, the loneliness of Donnelly sleeping rough on park-benches, his friendships with other writers, and the open, selfless propelling into political activity. It were as if Dublin represented one timescale; London and eventually Spain another. In a letter to his brother Tom, Donnelly remarks:

> And what grand people, simple, kindly, and intelligent. Like country people in Ireland. Only you feel that a great weight which they have borne for a long time has been thrown off and they feel the relief. You get a new impression that the entire community is involved in the business of organising public life, everybody interested and everybody enthusiastic. To go about among them gives you new courage—one day the Irish will be like this!

How his idealism would have coped with a return to the Ireland of the 40s it is difficult to know. As already suggested, there is the possibility that, towards the end of his life, Donnelly was becoming disillusioned with the Communist movement in Spain. We may never know. Certainly the time is ripe for a study that will re-examine the social, political and cultural conditions of the late 20s and 30s. For, as Joseph Donnelly aptly put it:

> It was a time when those who had nothing, had hope and those who had something, said their prayers. I can remember a maid of ours, named Lizzie, whose eyes would light up at the mention of de Valera's name. To her and to many others, de Valera had the answer to everything. This was the time of 'the great illusion'; we were back on the road to the Republic.

In reading Charles Donnelly's poems, one is forced back into considering "the time of "the great illusion'" and what became of *it.*

Such questions, of course, also lead on to other questions: about the viability of the Revival idealism and its afterglow in the late 20s and early 30s; the nature of republican socialism and its cultural modernism. They also make us uncomfortable with the dominant artistic image of the end of this period, which is Kavanagh trekking to Dublin in search of literary fame. While that image is consoling and in keeping with customary views of the Artist in Irish Society, the young intense Marxist discussing military history and strategy with the great military historian Liddell Hart, most certainly is not. In other words, Donnelly, like Coffey or Devlin, challenges our notions about what modern Irish literature is because, from well-off Catholic backgrounds, they reveal an Ireland and a literature unconducive to the official canon.

Writing of the pro-Franco Irish press, which he thought was scandalising the truth about the Spanish conflict, Donnelly had this to say:

> Didn't that section of the press ever remind you of beetles which scurry around when you lift a mossy stone and let in the light, fat, well-fed, and for all their middle-agedness, without the slightest knowledge of real life—except how to get the better of the next man.

Irish poets are not meant to speak like this or, if they do, they should be in full-flight in a bar somewhere. Donnelly meant it, though, and because of that, not only forfeited his life, but almost his claim to be considered a poet in the first place.

Whatever about the lost and/or misplaced poetry manuscripts, Donnelly's extant poems reveal an imagination fiercely at odds with its time. It is this critical edge which seems to me to be the keynote in much of what Donnelly wrote. Speculation as to what that imagination *might* have produced is as sterile and unjust to Donnelly's achievement as if one were to speculate on how Wilfred Owen's poetry would have developed had he survived the Great War, or Keith Douglas World War II.

Writing an obituary notice in *Left Review*, Montagu Slater commented that "latterly, Donnelly wrote about politics less, was writing verse, began a novel". Slater goes on to say that when Donnelly went to Spain, "in his last days [he] wrote a great deal of verse". This material has not emerged, despite the ceaseless attempts of his brother, Joseph, and Kay Donnelly to find it. Perhaps its fate mirrors the life of the young poet.

Poems are not just what is left, however; they are the beginning, middle and end of a very full story. For Donnelly packed so much in his 22 years. As he grew from the early poems of 'To You', 'At the

Dreaming of the Dreams', and 'Stasis', towards that deeper understanding I have only very briefly sketched in here, he proved himself a poet more than able to subject personal experience and intellectual passion to the imagination's will. While the scales were massed against his surviving Spain and the battle of Jarama, they cannot weigh against the fact that Charles Donnelly's poetry has survived.

5

Anatomist of Melancholia

Louis MacNeice

I remember one weekend, in 1968 or so, a school friend and I walked around Carrickfergus, his home town. I was not very impressed with the place. The day was clammy, the castle was, for all the world, like a sandcastle dissolving in the air. Coming down a sloping road, treelined with walled-in dripping hydrangeas, my friend said, "That's where the MacNeices lived". I cannot be sure of the details and I have never been back to Carrickfergus, but I see a silver plate on a stone gatepost and a half-view of a middle-class house, solid, stable and opaque. Such houses have always seemed fraught with grief, books, an unpleasant odour, cubby-holes, silence, mirrors, double-doors, slow diseases, unhappiness, confidence, tiredness, compassion, a terrible nostalgia and brown paint. It is MacNeice's world, one he bravely explored, because lurking there, in the stuffy cupboards, were often dangerous neuroses, fears and threats. MacNeice jokes about this in *The Strings Are False*:

> When we got home we would have tea in the nursery, strong tea thick with sugar, and sometimes before we went to bed, Miss Craig, for a treat, would give us thick beef sandwiches with mustard or a cold drink made from cream of tartar. Possibly our diet, though it was not the cause, was one of the conditions of my dreams. These got worse and worse. Where earlier I had had dreams of being chased by mowing-machines or falling into machinery or arguing with tigers who wanted to eat me I now was tormented by something much less definite, much more serious ... a grey monotonous rhythm which drew me in towards a centre as if there were a spider at the centre drawing in his thread and everything else were unreal.

In the poems, the dreams surfaced, or their occasions in his childhood, "calling back", as he wrote in 'Country week-end', from when:

> the soft lights marched
> Nightly out of the pantry and spread
>
> Assurance, not like the fickle candles
> Which gave the dark a jagged edge
> And made it darker yet, more evil,
> Whereas these lamps, we knew, were kind ...

What haunts MacNeice's poetry is what is strangely absent from *The Strings Are False*—his willingness to find out what lies in the corner of his mind: the dormant, flawed and mysterious feelings that pervade the poems. 'Aubade for Infants' hovers between the melodramatic and fearful: "I must spy what stalks behind/Wall and window./.../Beyond that wall what things befall?" and there is the fabulous poem 'Prayer Before Birth'. In *The Strings Are False,* MacNeice seems restricted, as if forthright prose was too crude, too obvious a medium for exploring his innermost thoughts. Only rarely does this happen, as when, for instance, in describing his school peers, he writes: "I could learn their language but they could not learn mine, could never breathe my darkness."

That "darkness", the fear and guilt which he associated with his disabled brother, hangs like a cloud over *The Strings Are False,* but the imaginative light by which MacNeice dispels it in his poems is absent. Perhaps one reason is simple, for *The Strings Are False* is not a particularly well-written book and it is unfinished.

MacNeice's prose style is fragmented, laboured in a restrained way, as if he was unsure of what to confide and of what should remain private. In effect, the book tells us little about the man. His attitude is abstracted, hesitant, irritable:

> The public schools of England have been written down *ad nauseum.* To flog these dying horses is no longer very daring and there have been more than enough autobiographies of rich boys faring ill, of sensitive plants wilting on the playing fields.

Indeed, there have been "enough autobiographies", but MacNeice's dismissal conceals his own ambiguity that is awkwardly couched in bravado in the concluding sentence of the paragraph just quoted: "As for the playing fields I for one never objected to them; to be rolled in the mud satisfied one of my instincts." This impulse, or device, to show just how ordinary and straightforward he was, like a neutral register of events and experience, can become tiresome in its middle-class understating of what often are life-changing priorities and decisions. Too often MacNeice writes of his life as if it were a game, yet we know that this is not the way he lived it: "For five months I had been tormented by the ethical problems of the war. In Ireland most people said to me 'What is it to you?'" This central ambivalence influences, perhaps even confuses, his autobiography in several ways: as regards Ireland and himself and the way he saw the intelligentsia of which he and his poetry were a part, to the skeletons that rattled away in his own past.

To take the first of these points, Ireland is a home for MacNeice's poetic imagination, but he reacts to it oddly, and his inconsistency can slip into sentimentality as when, thinking of his childhood, he recalls his father's writing-paper, "which came in boxes decorated with a round tower and an ancient Irish wolfhound; whenever I looked at this trademark I felt a nostalgia, sweet and melting, for the world where that wolfhound belonged".

Later, on a visit with his father to Omey Island, MacNeice comments:

> It was a country I had always known, mournful and gay with mournful and gay inhabitants, moonstone air and bloody with fuchsias. The mountains had never woken up and the sea had never gone to sleep and the people had never got civilised.

While the sentimentality is somewhat kept at a distance by the fact that MacNeice is recreating his sense of Ireland as a young man, there is this continuing contradiction: "I paid a flying visit to Dublin. I felt I was born again, to be able to go to Dublin on my own." But saved or not by Dublin's ease, MacNeice was to find himself isolated by its and the Free State's priorities:

> I was alone with the catastrophe [of World War II being declared], spent Saturday drinking in a bar with the Dublin literati; they hardly mentioned the war but debated the correct versions of Dublin street songs.

Throughout *The Strings Are False*, there seems to be a duality consisting of England, the ground upon which MacNeice feels he should prove himself, and Ireland, the place he wishes to be at home in. Constantly, the self-consciousness of this 'choice' intervenes, even when, as a young poet whose future looks relatively secure, he reminisces about Birmingham. Living there, he writes,

> ... had reconciled me to ordinary people; I found reassurance in silent gardeners, inefficient hospital nurses, in a golfer cupping a match in his hands in the wind, in business men talking shop in the train. I found no such reassurance in the intelligentsia.

Among the small circle of his friends, Auden obviously stands out in MacNeice's memory. It is for Auden that he writes one of the rare expressions of regard found in the book and even then it is qualified by an "at least":

> ... here at least was someone to whom ideas were friendly—they came and ate out of his hand—who would always have an interest in the world and always have something to say.

The uncertainty which I find to be the keynote of *The Strings Are False* is pervasive, and one comes across it as MacNeice charts his own experience always at twice a remove, externally:

> I continued dreaming about bombs and fascists, was worried over women, was mortifying my aesthetic sense by trying to write as Wystan did, without bothering too much with finesse, was bothering not to bother.

It is as if MacNeice was terrified of taking himself seriously, as if he felt he had no right to, and this, I feel, is due to his own fears about his past. For instance, like his contemporaries George Orwell and Albert Camus, MacNeice was haunted by the idea of death and yet he is reluctant to explore the reasons for this. Instead, he hesitates, turns it into a kind of literary question:

> It is better to be like Rilke and capitalise your own loneliness and neuroses, regard Death as the mainspring. Or it is better—if you can do it—to become the servant of an Idea.

Perhaps MacNeice felt that, as a poet, he lacked the intellectual and cultural tradition which could accept the viability of these questions, and consequently he was led, almost desperately, to turn against himself.

> Man cannot live by courage, technique, imagination—alone. He has to have a sanction from outside himself. Otherwise his technical achievements, his empires of stocks and shares, his exploitation of power, his sexual conquests, all his apparent inroads on the world outside, are merely the self-assertion, the self-indulgence, of a limited self that whimpers behind the curtains, a spiritual masturbation.

In passages such as this, MacNeice reveals more about himself than in the more ostensibly 'autobiographical' parts of the book. The almost puritan distaste that is represented there comes from, I believe, his own upbringing and the precarious place it had culturally and socially, in relating to either 'Ireland' of the wolfhound and tower or 'England' where Elizabeth his sister was sent, at 14, because "my stepmother thought it high time she should lose her Northern accent". In neither of these two places was MacNeice to find a natural stabilising support. He had to work at this, to *create* it, and it could well be that in doing so, he was, if not exactly resentful, at least unhappy that it could not have been otherwise.

Yet, when he writes of England, MacNeice's prose takes on a lyrical force absent from the almost caricatured image of Ireland.

> One May morning we were on this stretch of the Isis watching a dragonfly among the cow-parsley and shards on the bank when a goods train came over the railway bridge and we made a chant out of the names on the trucks—Hickleton, Hickleton, Hickleton, Lunt, Hickleton, Longbotham. This incantation of names at once became vastly symbolic—symbolic of an idle world of oily sunlit water and willows and willows' reflections and, mingled with the idleness, a sense of things worn out, scrap-iron and refuse, the shadow of the gas-drum, this England. Hickleton Hickleton Hickleton—the long train clanked and rumbled as if it had endless time to reach wherever it was going. The placid dotage of a great industrial country.

Such writing paints lasting images of the roots of imperial might, but MacNeice is also impressive, in the concluding passage of chapter XXVI, as he presents us with the first year of that mythologised decade—the 30s; decline is all around as MacNeice echoes the Dickens of *Bleak House*:

> Up in the industrial district on the north side of Birmingham the air was a muddy pond and the voices of those who expected nothing a chorus of frogs for ever resenting and accepting the *status quo* of stagnation.

Contrasted with passages like these, one finds that there are also memorable sentences of epigrammatic subtlety in *The Strings Are False*: "Clarification—it may be too much to demand of most people but a writer must demand it of himself"; "The armchair reformist sits between two dangers—wishful thinking and self-indulgent gloom."

Yet I come back to what I suppose can be called the tragic flaw of *The Strings Are False.* Here is MacNeice, again generalising, but beneath that cloak of abstractions, suggesting what is personally wrong:

> Man is essentially weak and he wants power; essentially lonely, he creates familiar daemons, Impossible Shes, and bonds—of race or creed—where no bonds are. He cannot live by bread or Marx alone; he must always be after the Grail.

That last impersonalised clause indicated his own search, lonely and without bonds, from an inherited religious legacy which sought for perfection even though, rationally, MacNeice knew it to be false. The emotional need was still there, nevertheless, unfulfilled by his creative self. Again he jokes about this, puts himself in the position of haughty disregard when, talking about his first marriage, he writes:

> I enjoyed metaphysics very much and hoped for a world-view. Whereas Mariette only hoped for a house of her own. But it will be possible, I thought, to achieve a compromise; I can live with Mariette in her house and still have a private wire to the cosmic outposts.

It is funny, MacNeice looking back on his utopian former self, but on the basis of *The Strings Are False* one is never sure if MacNeice found a workable compromise for his own life.

One thinks of his involvement in the Spanish Civil War, for instance. He was without question one of the most honest writers who went out to Spain and came back with his attitude to the left-wing politicians remaining consistently sympathetic, but sceptical. There was no failed political God for him and he lived by that light, avoiding, we can be thankful, those miserable recantations typical of many of his peers.

However, the image of Louis MacNeice I am left with is double-edged, twin-voiced: the uncertain, oppressed, doubting man of nightmares and the socialite drinker. A highly mannered style unites these two sides, creating poetry which is itself like a defence against himself, sometimes broached, giving us that distinctive mood of melancholia.

In MacNeice, I think we find the intellectual life at odds with itself, hurt by its acknowledgement of human imperfectibility and communicating this through lyrics of self-contemplation but always in acts of depreciation, lest the life is seen as a pose.

MacNeice is our anatomist of melancholia and it is with him that the truly deeper recesses of a northern Protestant upbringing are taken on, in spite of himself.

Perhaps MacNeice had this quotation from *Julius Caesar* in mind when he took the title of his autobiography from a phrase which shortly follows it:

> Brutus: ... it is the weakness of mine eyes
> That shapes this monstrous apparition.
> It comes upon me. Art thou any thing?
> Art thou some god, some angel, or some devil
> That mak'st my blood cold and my hair to stare?
> Speak to me what thou art.
>
> Ghost: Thy evil spirit, Brutus.

I think, though, of another Shakespearean figure, Hamlet, who like Brutus confronts the ghostly past, but also of the passage when he overcomes Guildenstern and Rosencrantz clucking for praise and gossip. It captures the quality of this poet's life, although MacNeice would have perished the thought, I am sure:

> I could be bounded in a nutshell and count
> myself a king of infinite space, were it
> not that I have bad dreams.

6

Against Piety

John Hewitt

> **colony** n.1. Settlement or settler in new country forming community fully or partly subject to mother State; their territory; people of one nationality or occupation in a city, esp. if living more or less in isolation or in a special quarter ... 2. (Gk. Hist.) independent city founded by emigrants; (Rom. Hist.) garrison settlement (usu. of veteran soldiers) in conquered territory.

I will not deal in any extensive way here with John Hewitt's poetry or, indeed, with the various motives and interpretations surrounding his changing views about regionalism and so forth. Instead, I want to consider the intersection, between the two phrases 'roots' and 'horizons' as they present themselves to me in a highly selective reading of Hewitt's work.

My connection with John Hewitt was mostly through correspondence, although I did meet him in the early 70s and his encouragement then was very important to me. I met him later at the occasional poetry reading in Belfast, but my understanding of John Hewitt has mostly been through his books, rather than through his personality. His was a presence formed in precise letters; not through regular contact. So I am intending now to explain to myself, publicly as it were, John Hewitt, a poet engaged by particular public and historical issues, the most central of which was his artistic and intellectual bearing on what being a writer might involve for someone, like myself, whose background was (is?) Protestant Belfast. So these are my main concerns: the public face of Hewitt's poetry, the 'Protestant' dimension of that and of how he seems to stand as a rather remote, isolated figure as regards both modern Irish and other literatures in English.

While he had anticipated many of the developments which have taken place in Irish poetry over the last 20 years, there always seemed to be about the man, as much as the poetry, a distance and reserve not solely temperamental in character. He rebuked the easy pieties of populist fashion and shadowed the cultural self-confidence of other Irish writers with an almost Victorian doubting. I felt that this distance had something specifically to do with his own sense of himself as a poet, reinforced by a curiously ambiguous expectation of, and reception for, the fact that he was, in some manner of speaking, a 'Protestant' writer from the 'Black North'; a strange fish, in other words.

I know I may be accused here of raising a hare while letting myself sit, to mix a mannered expression used in the Republic of Ireland where I have lived, worked and been a fully paid-up and taxed citizen for two decades. What is a 'Protestant writer', after all? By what peculiar gestures, accents, manicure, or space between his eyes, is this species known to man? I will pass this by and concentrate upon some of the features—the themes, attitudes, turn of voice—in Hewitt's work which make me think that there are relationships between these two terms 'Protestant' and 'writer', which run parallel to the terms 'roots' and 'horizons'.

For, in my own experience, I have been amazed by the complex and complicated tensions which link that background in Protestant Belfast (roots) with the world outside (horizons). Between these two poles of attraction and/or rejection, various images and caricatures, often absurd, sometimes funny, occasionally infuriating, intervene.

With Hewitt, the relationship was remarkably clear, stable and accessible. It was based upon his belief in a rational, reasonable world on which could be superimposed the dialectical decorum of art, both literary and visual, and maintained against the distortions and divisions of history itself.

John Hewitt: You have been asking whether we think our poetic role is analogous to Yeats's frequent public stand. Well I, for example, have written poems which are relevant to the political situation. Yet they are quoted in the *Irish Times* but not in the *Belfast Telegraph.* I am not speaking to my people. They are public utterances but they are taken up by a more distant audience than that for which they were intended.

Timothy Kearney: Is that an inescapable thing?

John Hewitt: Yes, it is inescapable thing. But linked with it is the important

> fact of the total lack of literary interest amongst unionists of the north, the lack of any fixed literary tradition.[1]

This ordering of Hewitt's "public utterances" is sharply focused by Edna Longley in a paper called 'Including the North'. The poetry, she writes, can be viewed from three angles: as cultural retrieval, defence and encounter based on local history and local artistic expression; as cultural self-criticism; and as an historical consciousness registering not only "seventeenth-and eighteenth-century events, but the First World War, the Easter Rising, the Second World War and other twentieth-century shocks and changes" deeply implicated in the poetry—to a further depth in poems written after 1968.[2]

It is to the substance of and attitude to these three aspects of Hewitt's writing that other critics will need to turn for an adequate account of his achievement, influence and example. I can merely gesture in that direction by raising what I hope are constructive questions.

II

One can, for example, turn to Hewitt's pioneering 1945 article, 'The Bitter Gourd: Some Problems of the Ulster Writer', to see how he linked the issues of 'roots' to the effect of boundless horizons. The Ulster writer, Hewitt states, "must be a *rooted* man, must carry the native tang of his idiom like the native dust on his sleeve; otherwise he is an airy internationalist, thistledown, a twig in a stream". And later he returns to this "question of rootedness", as he calls it himself:

> I do not mean that a writer ought to live and die in the house of his fathers. What I do mean is that he ought to feel that he belongs to a recognisable focus in place and time. How he assures himself of that feeling is his own affair. But I believe he must have it. And with it, he must have *ancestors*. Not just of the blood, but of the emotions, of the quality and slant of the mind.[3]

This passage is highly revealing of the "emotions, of the quality and slant" of Hewitt's mind, particularly when we align these statements with the central literary parallel which he draws in 'The Bitter Gourd'—New England and Robert Frost.

As a poet, Frost's "rural portraits are not alien to us", writes Hewitt, his "avoidance of ornament and rhetoric is kin to our logic, whose unhurried and sinewy wisdom is sympathetic to our highest moods". Against this 'rooted man', we can place a poem of Hewitt's, taken from Hewitt's best individual book, *The Rain Dance* (1978), 'On Reading Wallace Stevens' *Collected Poems* after many years':

Put this artificer of *chiaroscuro*
on the high shelf with all those phrase-bound poets,
padded with pedant's resonance, ballooned
with bouncing echoes of their paladins.

Give me, instead, the crisp neat-witted fellows,
sharp and laconic, making one word do,
the clipped couplet, the pointing syllables,
the clean-beaked sentence, the exact look.

Clearly Stevens, another New England man, is not rooted enough but enters the world as "an airy internationalist". This poem and what it implies is closely related to Hewitt's earlier statements about the Ulster writer being someone "who must be a *rooted* man" because that decision in itself is a gesture of appropriation, of domestication, of asserting one's self in one place, of becoming, as it were, a naturalised citizen. It has other implications, as well. Whereas "this artificer" Wallace Stevens is up to his eye-teeth in literariness ("a twig in the stream"), floating along impossible horizons, the neat-witted fellows have their feet squarely on the ground. In *The Rain Dance,* there are several poems singing such fellows' praises, as in 'William Conor, R.H.A. 1881-1968' and particularly the poem's opening lines:

So, Conor, take our thanks for what you've done
not through those harsh abstractions whose despair
of finding teeming earth forever fair
strip to a disc what we would face as sun,
nor lost in lonely fantasies which run
through secret labyrinths and mazes where
the dream-drenched man must find but few to share
the tortured forms his agonies have won.

There is though, in these phrases "lonely fantasies" and "secret labyrinths", a closing-off of possibility, a distinctive circumspection, to which I will return.

In Hewitt's example of New England and the reference to Robert

Frost in preference to Stevens, there is an interesting background to Hewitt's own view of himself as a rooted writer. For, as Robert Lowell remarked about Frost, "somehow [Frost] put life into a dead tradition" and, in a way, this was what Hewitt set himself to do in Ulster.

Indeed, like Robert Frost's, John Hewitt's poetry has itself become a cultural fact, involving one of the central themes of Irish life as much as of Irish literature. When Hewitt quotes Frost's 'The Gift Outright', he anticipates the last three lines of possibly his own most famous poem, 'The Colony':

> we would be strangers in the Capitol;
> this is our country also, no-where else;
> and we shall not be outcast on the world.

Who is "we"; which "Capitol"?; what "country"? In 'The Colony', and in many other poems, Hewitt has questioned that much abused concept, 'identity'. In 'Conacre', for instance, Hewitt writes:

> This is my home and country. Later on
> perhaps I'll find this nation is my own
> but here and now it is enough to love
> this faulted ledge ...

In that resolve, ("here and now it is enough to love"), the characteristic imaginative gesture in Hewitt's poetry is to be found: the roots. It is curious, though, to place alongside these lines of Hewitt's a passage from Seamus Heaney's 'Feeling into Words' (1974), roughly a quarter of a century after Hewitt's poem. In his lecture, Seamus Heaney takes up the notion of 'colony' in terms of the Roman *imperium*, a garrison settlement in conquered territory.

> I mean that I felt it imperative to discover a field of force in which, without abandoning fidelity to the processes and experience of poetry as I have outlined them, it would be possible to encompass the perspectives of a humane reason and at the same time to grant the religious intensity of the violence its deplorable authenticity and complexity. And when I say religious, I am not thinking simply of the sectarian division. To some extent the enmity can be viewed as a struggle between the cults and devotees of a god and a goddess. There is an indigenous territorial numen, a tutelar of the whole island, call her Mother Ireland, Kathleen Ní Houlihan, the poor old woman, the Shan Van Vocht, whatever; and her

> sovereignty has been temporarily usurped or infringed by a new male cult whose founding fathers were Cromwell, William of Orange and Edward Carson, and whose godhead is incarnate in a rex or caesar resident in a palace in London. What we have is the tail-end of a struggle in a province between territorial piety and imperial power.
>
> Now I realise that this idiom is remote from the agnostic world of economic interest whose iron hand operates in the velvet glove of 'talks between elected representatives', and remote from the political manoeuvres of power-sharing; but it is not remote from the psychology of the Irishmen and Ulstermen who do the killing, and not remote from the bankrupt psychology and mythologies implicit in the terms Irish Catholic and Ulster Protestant.[4]

The "tail-end of a struggle in a province between territorial piety and imperial power" is one way of contextualising what John Hewitt has written. The irony is that Hewitt's ambiguous relationship to the "imperial power" is founded *absolutely* upon "territorial piety". As he says in regard to 'The Colony', in 'No Rootless Colonist' (1972):

> I have not attempted to predicate by what means we may isolate the moment when a colony set among an older population ceases simply to be simply [sic] a colony and become something else, although I have not hesitated to take that 'something else' to be a valid *region* with the inalienable right to choose its place within a smaller or larger federation.

Hewitt's understanding of 'colony' looks more like its Greek root than the Roman: namely, an independent city founded by emigrants. And this is where the ideas of regionalism come in and the sense of ancestral voices and rootedness take on a radical dimension; because in both his poetry and prose, behind the seemingly low-keyed, formal determination, there is a belligerent doggedness to Hewitt ("as native in my thought as any here") very much in keeping with the community from which he came. After all, it is the "*sullen* Irish limping to the hills" in 'Once Alien Here' (my italics). While, in 'The Glens', Hewitt registers another old score in the disturbed northern mindfield: "I fear their creed as *we* have always feared/the lifted hand between the mind and truth" (my italics), later on revised for Alan Warner's edition of Hewitt's *Selected Poems* to "the lifted hand against unfettered thought".

Hewitt sees an "imperial power" closer to home than a "palace in London", yet there is a kind of awkward, self-conscious strain, the literariness of the city man perhaps, in much that he has written about the countryside, and those who live in it (strictly speaking, the barbarians). We detect it in the following poem, 'In the Rosses':

> The hospitable Irish
> come out to see who passes,
> bid you sit by the fire
> till it is time for mass.
>
> The room is bare, the bed
> is shabby in the corner,
> but the fine talk is ready
> and the wide hearth is warm.

The note of outsider-status feeding stereotypes here, in what Hewitt subtitled 'Scissors for a One-Armed Tailor', as *marginal* verses (1929-1954), should not be taken too much at face-value, because underlying it a very real uncertainty characterises his attitude to and understanding of the "hospitable Irish". While we can overlook the jaunting-car, tear-or-twinkle-in-the-eye postcard view, the trouble is in that "but" between the "bed ... shabby in the corner" and "the fine talk": quaint, oral consolations. There is too "time for mass". It is probably more just to say that in keeping with a man of his temperament and middle-class, suburban background, Hewitt may simply have had difficulty engaging with the human realities of actual impoverished country life. As several of his important poems show, the country, like the 'Irish', operated quite forcibly in Hewitt's mind at an abstract, intellectual level, and as a compensatory outlet for sensual, visual release.

This somewhat abstract quality, though, the sense of strain and putting on airs, has created an obstacle for already unsympathetic literary critics who are intent on 'placing' Hewitt in the canon of Irish poetry. The critical reception Hewitt has received as a poet in Britain, the Republic of Ireland, not to mention the United States, has been less than his due. On the one hand, he seems to be a more dowdy Edmund Blunden and hardly a suitable case for redbrick deconstruction. On the other hand, in the Republic, when on those rare occasions critical attention has actually travelled northwards, Hewitt stands as a reminder of the unassimilated Protestants. In this situation, Hewitt could have been more forthright in his address to the Republic of today rather than the ideal aspirations and hopes of republicans of two and more centuries ago.

His remarks in an interview in 1985 are appropriate here, when referring back to 'The Colony' as "the best statement of my point of view", he talks about his struggle for 50 years to sort out his own identity:

> I think I have a pretty clear grasp of it now. I couldn't, for instance, happily belong to a Gaelic-speaking Irish republic, because that's not my native tongue, and I don't want to separate it from Britain because the complete body, the corpus of my thought, has come from Britain. The ideas I cherish are British ideas ... my intellectual ancestry goes back to the Levellers at the time of Cromwell. England had become a republic, and they believed that people should be levelled, should be equal.[5]

This is a bit like having your 17th-century cake and eating it with your eyes closed three centuries later. What about applying the radical ideas, "strong British roots" and all, to the actual Republic on one's doorstep? Hewitt is less than enamoured of the prospect: "... there were no Irish Levellers, no Irish Diggers. The Irish people before my ancestors came here, were a tribe of cattle-rustlers, fighting each other and burning churches and what not. They wrote very nice songs and somewhat good poetry. I'd like to include them too in the general picture, but they're not the whole of the story."

'They', of course, are not "the whole of the story", but who ever is? There is the strongest whiff here of a defensiveness turned, under the informality of an interview, into fighting talk. And needless to say, this is very important in itself because it relates to one of the crucial issues John Hewitt represents. For his poetry attempts to find practicable resolutions to what history has given him by way of a home, a family's past and the 'natural' cultural world into which he was born. The word 'resolution' implies not only something determined upon as an act of faith, but also an assurance to keep going, no matter what; the need to bear witness. The first sense invokes the making of a myth; the second involves personal integrity and an artistic single-mindedness. Both senses are revealed in how the poetry itself is made. Perhaps this does not amount to a vision, but when one looks around at poetry in the English language today, one must ask: how many other poets have come as near as Hewitt to creating a vision for himself and for others to live by?

III

Taken as a whole, Hewitt's poetry provides a myth and one that is not circumscribed by the immediate experience of Irish history. Indeed, Hewitt's poetry can be viewed in a different light which reflects upon the actual homelessness of modern man. I am not suggesting that his poetry is allegorical in any conscious, forthright manner, but that in its constant focusing upon the present and in its romantic attachments to the past, in the description of certain places during certain times (the Glens of Antrim, Belfast, Coventry and Greece, during various periods ranging from the early 20s to the present), and in the portraits he gives us of poets, craftsmen and his own descendants, Hewitt defines the tenuous grasp we effectively have on the 'real' world. His poetry actually argues that we must make a conscious effort to decide who and what we are (establishing 'roots'), rather than accepting an identity imposed from without. The ambivalent attitude to the country people ("You are coarse to my senses/to my washed skin") and his acknowledgement of his own 'separateness' ("I found myself alone who had hoped for attention") are marks of a man at least unwilling to acquiesce in the domination of the past. He has, as it were, been pushed reluctantly to make his own way in the prodigal world. The reluctance is shown in Hewitt's antipathy towards artists such as Wallace Stevens whom, as I have already mentioned, he sees as making a virtue out of what is an unwelcome and possibly disabling state—having to find a language in which the writer can report back on his experiences to those who are willing to listen "across a roaring hill". Those experiences are condensed in the relationship between Hewitt's myth-making and his sense of restraint in dealing with the ambition of his art. It is a restraint that can cause problems for the reader more accustomed to a provocative art, and lends itself, perhaps a little too readily, to quotation and paraphrase.

In the articles he wrote for *The Bell* in 1953 as 'Planter's Gothic: An Essay in Discursive Autobiography', writing under the name of John Howard, Hewitt traces his family's past and notes laconically that not having been baptised gave him "a sense of liberation, spiritually I have felt myself to be my own man, the ultimate Protestant". Perhaps taking his cue from this remark, John Montague, in an article called 'Regionalism into Reconciliation: The Poetry of John Hewitt' (1964), referred to Hewitt as the "first (and probably the last) *deliberately*

Ulster, Protestant poet".[6] But both the autobiographical gloss and Montague's description are a little misleading for it seems to me that Hewitt's poetry expresses the *contradiction* between a "sense of liberation", be that spiritual or not (horizons), and the claims that a specific form of Protestant faith, Methodism, made upon him (his 'roots').

For while the temper of Hewitt's poetry is often one of dissent, from the orthodoxies of his own past as much as that of "a vainer faith/and a more violent lineage" (the "creed" he fears in 'The Glens'), there is always a counter-aesthetic which restrains him. It could be described best in Isaac Watts' terms: "because I would neither indulge any bold metaphors, nor admit hard words, nor tempt the ignorant worshipper to sing without his understanding." This is the reasonable liberal light by which we should read Hewitt's poetry. Donald Davie says in *A Gathered Church* (1978), from which source the Watts quotation comes, that the "aesthetic and the moral perceptions, have, built into them and near to the heart of them, the perceptions of license, of abandonment, of superfluity, foreseen, even invited and yet in the end denied, fended off". For what better way is there to view one of the more significant features of Hewitt's poetry than to see in it the struggle against art's enticement, the lure of the imagination, distant horizons, the unknown—and the need to resist this in both poetic and political terms. Hewitt writes of this tension convincingly, implicitly, but rarely do we see such a personal stating of it as we do in one of his finest achievements, 'Sonnets for Roberta (1954)', with their calm, almost Shakespearean poise:

I have let you waste
the substance of your summer on my mood;
the image of the woman is defaced,
and some mere chattel-thing of cloth and wood
performs the household rites, while I, content,
mesh the fine words to net the turning thought.
or eke the hours out, gravely diligent,
to draw to sight that which, when it is brought,
is seldom worth the labour.

or in 'The Faded Leaf: a chapter of family history':

I know that grave, the headstone; the text

I am proud of, for its honesty:
We all do fade as a leaf: no easy hope,
no sanctimonious, Pentecostal phrase,
simply a natural image for the fact.
I've written verses of the falling leaf.

As he wrote in *The Bell* (July 1952), discussing possible attitudes open to the writer in modern society, the one of "rarefication" led to a "withdrawal from the community, from the day-to-day, from the topic of the time, into memories of childhood, nostalgia, the pastoral, the slightly fantastic, the rather obscure, accompanying this, a deliberate modification of technique, a narrowing of focus, a magnification of detail, a meticulous searching for precision in phrase and image, an increased preciosity. This way so much is left out ...". And while he remarks later, "I am not decrying all work in this mode", we can clearly sense his disapproval of such work since the assumed responsibility of art in the writer's community is neglected, which results in "increased preciosity" in the writing.

To balance these different demands seems to be Hewitt's overriding concern and he has achieved this by concentrating his imaginative energies upon that theme referred to earlier in 'The Colony'. For Hewitt has founded a myth within which these conflicts between art and morality, imaginative release and self-restraint, roots and horizons, are absorbed and transcended. This myth concerns his relationship as a Protestant or Dissenter to Ireland's past, the disputed territory of land that Hewitt metaphorically possesses through identifying with its natural beauty, the landscape of a place "irremediably home". To what extent this myth has narrowed Hewitt's poetic appeal, or limited the imaginative scope of his work, is open for debate. He has, however estranged himself from the other perceptions made of the common Irish inheritance, acknowledged the conflicting versions of history in his country and embodied these in his poetry. On occasion, he sees his own myth-making ironically, as in 'Away Match: June 1924', when recollections of his boyhood are checked: "Idyllic the setting: the myth spored from paper;/our school-story values never were true". But in major poems like 'An Irishman in Coventry', 'The Scar', 'The Glens' and 'Clogh-Oir', he weds his personal life to "all the past foregathered" and instructs us with that imaginative union.

Such poems, like much of his prose, have encouraged critics to look at Hewitt's work solely in terms of regionalism. He has, indeed, at various stages drawn attention to this very issue. From the 1952 'Writing in Ulster' article published in *The Bell*, for instance, to his afterword in Judith C. Wilson's *Conor: 1881-1968*, Hewitt discussed the viability of a regional culture and its provincial virtues, but always bearing in mind the status of the artist, considering what other options may be open to him or her. Yet, it must be said, these options like 'exile' are of only abstract interest to Hewitt. In 'Conversations in Hungary, August, 1969', the poet finds that his country's past catches up with him as if it were his fate. His host asks:

> You heard the bulletin?
> And added, with no pause for our reply;
> Riots in Northern Ireland yesterday:
> and they have sent the British Army in.

In this, one of Hewitt's more free-formed poems, the confidence of the lines, the conversational ease, are drawn up against the reality they allude to:

> ... we turned to history:
> the savage complications of our past;
> our luckless country where old wrongs outlast,
> in raging viruses of bigotry,
> their first infection ...

and in the "ironic zest" of his host, Hewitt poses the European experience of war as a backdrop to Ireland's violence, "Between two factions, in religion's name",

> Your little isle, the English overran—
> our broad plain, Tatar, Hapsburg, Ottoman—
> revolts and wars uncounted—Budapest
> shows scarce one wall that's stood two hundred years.
> We build to fill the centuries' arrears.

Yet Hewitt neither despairs nor opts for the enlightened pain or wounds to which some critics "attach a very high degree of spiritual prestige" (to use Lionel Trilling's phrase). Instead, as he says, "he mourns for his mannerly verses/that had left so much unsaid" ('A Local Poet').

IV

Much is always left unsaid. Poets can only ever write the kind of poems they alone write. In his contribution to the *Fortnight* Supplement on John Hewitt (July-August 1989), Terence Brown has accurately identified an impulse in John Hewitt's writing that was not sufficiently explored: "[Hewitt] established a certain range of tones and poetic manners early on and although his work accumulated impressively it did not seem to deepen or change in any fundamental way. But in [his poem] 'Man Fish and Bird' one senses another dimension to this poet's imagination, his shadow."

It seemed as if that other dimension led to those "secret labyrinths and mazes", of the "dream-drenched man" which in his poem to William Conor, Hewitt dismissed as an indulgence: the perceptions of license and abandonment which Hewitt was chary of and mostly avoided in his poetry for a sharper, more publicly accessible verse. It is here, too, that John Hewitt strikes me as being an important, *the* important, bridge between poet and audience. With time, the proper dimension of his work will be weighted by the necessary checks and balances of literary criticism. Be that as it may, Hewitt's legacy is in his poems, not in the polemical awareness he sought to find in response to the political questions the sorry state of Northern Ireland provoked. If this legacy did not include an opening-up to other literary traditions and horizons (European and otherwise), it has *established* a moral context for younger writers to honour. I think this is the personal legacy that John Hewitt handed on and it is visible in the persistence and graciousness of Michael Longley, as well as in the researches of John Wilson Foster and Frank Ormsby. Hewitt also rebukes those who insist (or, more cunningly, assume) that Protestants have in some way to prove their Irishness.

For me, ultimately (and selfishly), John Hewitt's greatest, and simplest, contribution has been to reassert the possibility of actually having 'roots' in a Belfast Protestant background that will not necessarily lead to the stranglehold of bigotry, or half-baked and ludicrously gentrified 'Anglo' self-images. Given the desired artistic resources, poems and plays and novels *could* come from such a background—if not *should* come, for Hewitt always resisted the imperative view of poetry being written to order.

John Hewitt also reminds us of the primacy of politics in a divided culture having the responsibility to 'solve' its problems. He was an activist in this sense. Literature cannot take up that burden, but can offer itself instead as something which, to an exhausted and frustrated people, overcomes those problems momentarily and provides a kind of new idiom, an imaginative space. For when one thinks of the enormous problems faced by a writer like Nadine Gordimer in South Africa, or the decay and collapse of their language which German writers such as Günther Grass and Heinrich Böll experienced in the years after World War II, it makes one wonder how, in the infinitely less oppressed, yet paramilitarised, atmosphere of Ireland today, the writers, readers and teachers of literature have not had a greater influence on the predicted course of events over the last two decades.

Cultural debate, such as that which John Hewitt to a large degree initiated, can well anticipate or even inspire political action. But it cannot be a substitute for political action. Poetry in Ireland is mostly an accepted form of the tradition, and most poets in Ireland voice ideas and beliefs totally at one with official cultural orthodoxies. Consequently, the forum that cultural discussion provides is always, and can only be, an alternative one, that must fail *unless* the civic space of political acts and responsibilities is made publicly available and accessible in institutional form. There is no way around this. What has happened over the last number of years in the north is that, in keeping with experience in England, this space has shrunk. In Ireland, there are fragments of different historical nations—English, Scottish and Irish, with other floating sects and religious residues such as the French Huguenots. Elevated above these fragments, we have been asked to subscribe to one or other stereotypical images of 'Ireland' or 'England', without any real purchase on what such images actually mean, in economic, social or cultural terms, to the people involved.

All this is, of course, sociological, and why should a poet or literary critic be concerned with it, when it will be thrown back in his or her face by the experts as unscientific or speculative? Yet public prominence is given to writers in Ireland (and Irish writers abroad) on the basis of these very contexts and not primarily on the nature and quality of their writing.

It is necessary to disengage the creative and critical preoccupation with, on the one hand, an imagined place and moral demands of justice, and, on the other, the experience of a people deemed by history to be oppressors, as the Protestants from northern Ireland are cast worldwide. A task which has very little in common with the calculators of identity crises who purvey ready-made answers and anxieties; it remained an obsessive burden from which Hewitt sought, with enlightenment and modesty, to deliver his community.

It was with that selfless commitment in mind that John Hewitt wrote his poems and essays; against the grain, a lot of the time and also, against piety. As he wrote in 'Ars Poetica':

> So be the poet. Let him till his years
> follow the laws of language, feeling, thought,
> that out of his close labour there be wrought
> good sustenance for other hearts than his.
> If no one begs it, let him shed no tears,
> five or five thousand—none will come amiss.

Notes

[1] An interview entitled 'Beyond the Planter and the Gael', *The Crane Bag* 4.2 (1980-1), pp. 722-29.

[2] 'Including the North', *Texts and Contexts* 3 (1988), pp.17-24.

[3] Unless otherwise indicated, references to Hewitt's writing are taken from *The Selected John Hewitt*, ed. Alan Warner (Belfast: Blackstaff, 1981), *Collected Poems 1932-67* (London: MacGibbon and Kee, 1988) and *Ancestral Voices: The Selected Prose of John Hewitt*, ed. Tom Clyde (Belfast: Blackstaff, 1987). Subsequently, *The Collected Poems of John Hewitt*, edited by Frank Ormsby (Belfast: Blackstaff, 1992).

[4] *Preoccupations: Selected Prose 1968-1978* (London: Faber, and Faber, 1980), pp.56-7.

[5] *Fortnight* (February, 1985).

[6] *Poetry Ireland*, repr. in John Montague, *The Figure in the Cave and Other Essays* (Dublin: Lilliput, 1989), pp. 147-53.

[7] *A Gathered Church* (London: Routledge & Kegan Paul, 1978), p.26.

7

Our Secret Being

Padraic Fiacc

I

Padraic Fiacc has been publishing for almost 50 years. The unmistakable shape and sound of his poems have found a lasting artistic echo in the personal and social traumas of his own life and times. That this poetry radically subverts what we often expect to see and hear in a poem is clear from the outset of *Ruined Pages: Selected Poems of Padraic Fiacc* (1994). The collection is intended to serve as an introduction to Fiacc's work—from the earliest surviving poems of the 40s to those of the present—and also includes *Hell's Kitchen*, Fiacc's account of the autobiographical and cultural sources of his writing.

The poetry of Padraic Fiacc departs from the Gaelic otherworld of myth and folklore before settling in the uncharted territory that is Belfast's violent history. It is a story, told with fantastic realism and melodramatic relish, which anticipates many of the most hotly debated issues of contemporary life and literature.

Fiacc's work is preoccupied with language as a physically despoiled body—the violated page, the exploded word-order. There has been much talk of late about the theme of inner exile and the use of dialect as a means of refurbishing the jaded artistic persona and poetic of contemporary literature in English. Here, too, Fiacc's work is central, for no figure of the Poet could be more isolated and more aware of the fact than Fiacc himself, while his poems are obsessed with the actual word-ordering and depth-charged nuances of common speech.

Fiacc's ability to use idiomatic phrasing and cliché is a marvellous illustration of one of his poetry's main values. Similarly, the voice that in 'A Slight Hitch' describes the "ghost-faced boy-broadcaster" who breaks down, "(can you imagine, and him/'live' on the TV screen!)", is drawn against "the usual cold, acid/and dignified way" of the "NORTHERN IRELAND BRITISH/BROADCASTING CORPORATION". This linguistic battle for authenticity, at the very heart of Fiacc's poetry, aligns him with the work of Tony Harrison and other 'Barbarian' poets of today. It is a verbal dexterity also paralleled by the imagery of his poetry, like the opening of 'More Terrorists':

> The prayer book is putting on fat
> With *in memoriam* cards.
>
> The dead steal back
> Like snails on the draining board
>
> Caught after dark
> Out of their shells.

Throughout Fiacc's work, the pervasive sense of childhood (of the poet's own childhood, of his daughter's and, in a bizarre way, of the city's) cuts up against the deadly inheritance of sectarian hatred and violence, "crossing our stunted lives", as he writes in 'Glass Grass'. It is the ordinary lives that are stripped of stability and forced instead to live with fear:

> She said she saw a man's head pass by
> The second-storey window.
>
> 'Och notatall granma
> Or else he'd be an awful long
> John Silver!'
>
> Then the lamp was hurled
> And geranium pot after geranium pot
> Before whoever it was could
> Find her a bed in the asylum from
> Childhood to childhood, in a world
> -womb to womb: to womb removed.

This comes from 'Dark Night of the Mill Hag' and there are other similar portraits, like the Kafkaesque 'Dirty Protest', which asks how life ever became so broken: "Blown up, thrown down born alive."

The intellectual legacy that shadows Fiacc's poetry draws upon a classic Catholic one, turned on its head and spliced with modernism, as Pascal, Mauriac, Baudelaire and Joyce coalesce in Fiacc's troubled imagination. There is, too, a wry, terse, almost despairing humour reminiscent of John Berryman, as in 'Intimate Letter 1973':

> Our Paris part of Belfast has
> Decapitated lamp posts now. Our meeting
> Place, the Book Shop, is a gaping
> Black hole of charred timber.

Fiacc can also blend these poetic skills into a beautiful poignant lyric, such as 'Goodbye to Brigid/an *Agnus Dei*', with its opening evocation of Belfast offering up the unforgettable plea:

> My little girl, my Lamb of God,
> I'd like to set you free from
> Bitch Belfast as we pass the armed
>
> -to-the-back-teeth barracks and
> Descend the road into the school
> Grounds of broken windows from
>
> A spate of car-bombs, but
> Don't forgive me for not.

II

Padraic Fiacc's poetry traces his imagination's troubled and broken course through the impounding claims of Irish history and mythology. Chronologically, *Ruined Pages* charts Fiacc's engagement with both these forces—a process marked by personal idealism, and then disillusionment which finally breaks down, recoiling from any such 'logic', withdrawing from possibility itself into the "depths of our dark/Secret being" ("Credo Credo').

Up to and including 'First Movement', the poems from Fiacc's first published collection, *By the Black Stream* (Dolmen, 1969), are written with a clear conception of the Irish monastic style. Sharp, syntactical inversions, bright colours, and sense of the world as a natural wonder against which man is a sort of tragicomic intrusion: these traditional features conceal the stolen joy of the poet in the world.

Yet these innocent perceptions seem to exist in spite of the encroaching strain of the world, of experience threatening to stain the poet's consciousness, and it is here that the jagged thrust of Fiacc's imagery takes over. 'Der Bomben Poet 1941' strangely anticipates Fiacc's poetic fate in this regard. The more disharmonious nature is seen to be, the more discordant and unpredictable the world, the more the poet tries to cast images in chaotic likeness, as in 'The ghost':

> Out of bull resentment
> Snores to the moon
> At black nightfall
>
> By my side a skull
> Hunted Dermot down:
>
> In all the land the lack
> Of what was whole ...

Poems like 'Master Clay', 'Lives of a Student', 'Themes from a Gloss' and 'Alive Alive O' are tuned into each other. This complementary process becomes disturbed and disjointed, however, at quite an early point, as in 'First Movement'. Fiacc is obviously aware of the importance of this poem since he has brought it into two collections, marking points of hesitancy and anticipation of change. The poem is also noticeable for its accomplished simplicity and the characteristic contrasting of urban with natural imagery:

> I was born on such a morning
> Smelling of the Bone Yards
>
> The smoking chimneys over the slate roof tops
> The wayward storm birds

But the following passage is particularly relevant here:

> And to the east where morning is, the sea
> And to the west where evening is, the sea

Threatening with danger

And it would always darken suddenly.

That sudden darkening and threatening with danger is the first key perception which Fiacc makes of his disintegrating relationship with the world around him. 'First Movement' demonstrates the characteristic style in which Fiacc's poems circle to the source of danger and threat; stunned by the sudden eruption of buried energies and forces that obliterate danger (which is immanent, an exposure to harm) with the deluge of reality. It is for this uncompromising recognition that Fiacc is best known, as he wryly says in 'Glass Grass':

My fellow poets call my poems 'cryptic, crude, dis
-tasteful, brutal, savage, bitter ...'

The tempestuous reputation that is all too often associated with Fiacc's poetry is deduced from the "brutal, savage, bitter". Yet such a reading is one-sided because it fails to account for the sources of Fiacc's poetry, or to describe the technical skills he brings to his writing.

The general impression given by Fiacc's work is one of entrapment: man is held in a painful stasis, pinned between the past and the future and, in this vision, images drawn from religion and impoverished social conditions coalesce. One of the most powerful physical images of this stasis can be found in 'Internee':

And it does not hurt
To be jeered at

When you are hanging
Upside down,

When hanging upside down hurts more.

As a cumulative condition, it is compounded of a range of imaginative experience. For instance, Fiacc's own experience of Ireland as the conflict between an ideal world and terrible reality is a persistent theme in his poetry. In 'Icon', Ireland is the cause and effect of the individual's entrapment:

Unholy mother Ireland banging
on the wall in labour
...
We were born in her

Screams to 'Get Out!'

But if Ireland is seen as a mother giving birth, in 'Fire Light' the life given is interpreted with existential despair:

... in this so strange
'So Be It Now' as if

It never really were
Or never will be

Only always is.

Fiacc constantly stresses an enclosed, trapped world; one where "We all run away from each other's/Particular hell" ('Intimate Letter 1973') and the force that superintends the hell has an absolute stature in 'Our Father':

The evil thing being
That which crushes us.

Fiacc rarely attempts to overcome the darkness, but in 'The Fall' he makes the gestures of rebellion:

It's vengeance I want
But vengeance on whom?

It is as if Fiacc refuses to acknowledge this life; our being is corrupt, and his poetry speaks of the disintegrated ontology we have inherited with all its vast psychic (as much as social) injustice. But if Fiacc's work operates on this level in general, the poems deal with specific and identifiable onrushes of reality: the oppressive 'military machine', the deprived environment of a discarded working class, or the impact of mythology on everyday life, as in 'Elegy in "the Holy Land"':

O dolly-Eurydice, my dark Ros

-aleen dream
                    of bog on bog of bone
-grounded cloud, Ireland, my dear

Dragon seed pod ...

Most poignantly, this sense of failure resides in family-life, where the contradiction between dream and reality is most acute, as in the imagery of 'Goodbye to Our Father':

                    I see your bone-naked
Face scrutinising 'Injustices' still!

Never bother! You have a hole to hide
                    in now ...

If there is no release from the entrapment, if there are no ways out, Fiacc can also see the black humour of being there. He does this through self-dramatisation and by the use of the aggressive understatements of Belfast vernacular speech.

Fiacc's poetry deals with the urban landscape and, in this, he separates himself again from the general drift of Irish poetry. With its bases in rural landscapes—decayed, mythic or desolate—and its metaphoric wells sunk far from "the damp down by the half-dried river/Slimy at night on the mud flats" ('Haemorrhage'), Irish poetry has tended to evade the city as imaginatively hostile or indifferent. In 'The Black and the White', Fiacc strikes the exact note of city life, the hostility is embraced, the empty night-time streets, the loneliness, violence and loss:

Sinking on iron streets, the bin-lid
-shielded, battleship-grey-faced kids

Shinny up the lamp post, cannot tear
Themselves away, refuse to come in

From the dying lost day ...

It is not that city life is a contagion; in 'Our Fathers', it is infected by industrial wastefulness:

A grey cloud of pollution from Power

Chimneys, mill house, laundries, cars.

When this environment is seen to be born of a corrupting past, the violent present spreads through every perception, affecting it with an inevitable meaning that imposes itself, like the remorseless rain, on our consciousness, as in 'The Wrong Ones':

The howl of the rain beating on the military tin
Roof is like the tolling of a bell
Tolling for a childhood more
Murdering than murdered.

I rise and stalk across the scarred with storm
-erected daisies, night in the north, grass.

Throughout Fiacc's poetry, and in his past commentaries upon it and upon literature in general, there runs a deep hostility to the paraphernalia of art. Fiacc's Beckettian anti-art abandon caustically overthrows, so to speak, the pretentiousness of art, while cauterising the poet's own unavoidable and reckless bonds with life. Fiacc's sense of himself as a poet is, accordingly, both mocking and tragic.

The often ugly parasitic relationship between literature and its immediate or historical world of suffering can, in Fiacc's book, lead to a neutralising of that suffering. Literature seems to stabilise the violence by drawing it into its own circuit of imaginative ordering. In the lived world, the suffering continues to overwhelm. Such contradictions and ambiguities cannot be left out of the picture, because they are part of the imaginative process: to excise them damages and destroys the terrible truthfulness that Fiacc's poetry struggles to articulate, for his poems dramatise the human effects of moral and psychological decay upon the lives of the ordinary people for whom, and of whom, he speaks. Time after time, his poetry points to the erosion of human potential, and the indictment is laid at the door of the political establishment.

No other poet writing in Ireland today has been so forthright and committed in saying the uncomfortable thing. Padraic Fiacc is the first of Belfast's poets to have imaginatively possessed, with such unremitting intensity, not only his own life, but the life of his profoundly troubled city as well. It is an extraordinary and disturbing achievement.

8

Blood and Family

Thomas Kinsella

I

The first series of Peppercanister poems which Thomas Kinsella published through his own press began with *Butcher's Dozen* in 1972 and included *A Selected Life, Vertical Man* (1972, 1973) and *The Good Fight* (1973). These were followed by the second series: *One* (1974), *A Technical Supplement* (1976) and *Songs of the Night and Other Poems* (1978). The third series contained *The Messenger* (1978), *Songs of the Psyche* and *Her Vertical Smile* (both 1985). The fourth series opened with *Out of Ireland* and *St. Catherine's Clock* (both 1987). All 12 individual sequences published by Kinsella were subsequently issued in trade editions as *Peppercanister Poems 1972-1978* (Wake Forest, 1979), which gathered everything up to and including *The Messenger,* while *Fifteen Dead* and *One and Other Poems* (both from Dolmen/OUP, 1979) collected the original seven sequences. OUP have also published *Blood and Family* (1988) which contains the Peppercanister sequences from *The Messenger* to *St. Catherine's Clock.*[1]

This somewhat cluttered bibliographical introduction tells its own story. Since the mid-70s, Kinsella seems to have moved away from the more conventional publishing record of his slightly younger Irish contemporaries in which a new book of poems appears approximately every three years. This fact alone underlies an important aspect of Thomas Kinsella's work as a poet, because in the Peppercanister series, and in the earlier books which established his reputation, such as *Another September* (1958), *Downstream* (1962) and *Nightwalker and Other Poems* (1968), Kinsella has persistently checked and double-backed on himself, questioning all the time the forms of his art.

There is no predictable thematic seam that the reader or critic can readily extract from Kinsella's poetry; by its very nature, it challenges such consolations. He is too, as Hugh Kenner called T.S. Eliot, an invisible poet, even when his poems deal most directly with family life or the quickest sense of his 'self'. Kinsella is elsewhere, working the poems: "I would rather settle for the facts and let them speak among themselves"[2], he remarked in an interview. "I don't think graceful postures are adequate; you have to deal with the raw material."[3]

This sense of an uncompromising artistic confrontation lies behind much of the Peppercanister poetry. It is very close to another facet of Kinsella's imagination which he identified comparatively early in his writing (1959): "I could never honestly see how anybody, even the most Romantic of poets, could escape the bonds of hard work which man must face as a result of Adam's sin."[4] More than twenty years later, interviewed by John Haffenden, Kinsella speaks of his writing in the following terms:

> ... the poetry I've most recently finished is part of a continuing investigation into the given human beings in my past—parents and grandparents—who seem to me very valuable instances, and to have undergone some very positive as well as negative experiences. The poetry is growing, I think, in response to these things.[5]

The "bonds of hard work" and a phrase like "continuing investigation" should alert us to the creative principle upon which Kinsella's work as a poet stands. It suggests not so much determinism—although *A Technical Supplement* could be faulted for its excessively forced self-consciousness—but rather his commitment to explore, probe and understand the present without any guaranteed *a priori* literary form with its assumed moral and social order to rely upon. This commitment, or responsibility as Kinsella would call it, gives the poetry an almost take-it-or-leave-it aggressiveness unique in Irish poetry.

Kinsella has spoken of his debt to Ezra Pound's *Cantos* and to William Carlos Williams, but the more accessible comparison to bear in mind, for present purposes, is with Robert Lowell. Like Kinsella, Lowell's poetry draws heavily and persistently upon the emotional and cultural inheritance of his family, and, through them, his country. (Only in this profounder sense can Kinsella be called a 'national' poet.) Perhaps Kinsella has this in mind when, in his contribution to 'Poetry since Yeats: An Exchange of Views', he noted "in American poetry a seriousness that is fruitful, and that is embodied [in] William Carlos Williams' last poetry and Robert Lowell's public progress".[6] Kinsella goes on to discuss briefly the change of idiom between Lowell's *Mills of the Kavanaughs* (1951) and *Life Studies* (1959) as "a notable achievement":

> Lowell's subsequent re-positioning, a lucky relaxation of effort and the finding of an easier level, is a high technical achievement—and, I repeat, instructive. The ability to make this change, and the general, quick, sensitive realisation by Lowell's audience that it mattered, imply for me an alertness in the atmosphere in which the change occurred. It gives a sense of possibility and expectation. The scene has the groping characteristics of growth: multitudinous individual effort, frequent adjustments and failures, uncorrupted movements; with an unusually high level of sensitiveness.[7]

Spoken over 20 years ago, nevertheless the note of hesitant expectation is unmistakable and it relates generally to the freeing of Kinsella's own work into the haunting panoramic vision of *Nightwalker* or the penultimate image around which 'Ritual of Departure' closes:

> I saw the light
> Enter from the laneway, through the scullery
> To the foot of the stairs, creep across grey floorboards,
> Sink in plush in the staleness of an inner room.

From this emblematic moment in Kinsella, it is a short step into the fuller realisations of 'Hen Woman', 'A Hand of Solo', 'The High Road', 'Ancestor', 'Tear' and 'Irwin Street' (*Notes from the Land of the Dead*, 1973)—poems which Kinsella called "completely exploratory".[8]

At roughly this time too, the early 70s, the first Peppercanister series came into public view, characterised by a complete loosening, or "re-positioning of effort" on Kinsella's behalf, ranging from the aggrieved polemic of *Butcher's Dozen* to the fond memorialising of Seán O Riada in *A Selected Life* and *Vertical Man* and his poem in tribute to John F. Kennedy, *The Good Fight*.

II

With *One and Other Poems*, Kinsella moved more immediately into the imaginative contexts that have dominated his own poetry for the last decade or more. In '38 Phoenix Street', for instance, we see the *dramatis personae* of family; the primeval landscape; the marooned objectifiable 'self'—all fixed in place by the childlike eye of perception that experiences everything from the minutest organism to the monumental scales of history in their own untranslatable terms of reference:

> Look.
>   The other. Looking.
> My finger picked at a bit of dirt
> on top of the wall and a quick
> wiry redgolden thing
> ran back down a little hole.

While 'Mister Cummins' becomes in the poem almost thing-like under the literal weight of one man's random fate:

> A black rubbery scar stuck on his white forehead.
>
> Sealed in his sad cave. Hisshorror erecting
> slowly out of its rock nests, nosing the air.
> He was buried for three days under a hill of dead,
> the faces congested down all round him
> grinning *Dardanelles!* in the dark.
>
> They noticed him by a thread of blood
> glistening among the black crusts on his forehead.
> His heart gathered all its weakness, to beat.
>
> A worm hanging down, its little round
> black mouth open. Sad father.

One searches for some definite origin, a place to begin from, a true bearing, but at each possible stopping-off point throughout the sequence (a recollection; a landscape; a portrait), an impatient narrative voice insists, "Beyond that". Beyond the family history and the religious upbringing and the available celebrations like traditional music, a relentless hunger for beginnings presents itself, disembodied and unexpectedly in dream, or at those moments of dangerous uncertainty:

> We steered in along a wall of mountain
> and entered a quiet hall of rock echoing
> to the wave-wash and our low voices.
> I stood at the prow. We edged to a slope of stone.
> I steadied myself. 'Our Father ... ', someone said
> and there was a little laughter. I stood
> searching a moment for the right words.
> They fell silent. I chose the old words once more
> and stepped out. At the solid shock
> a dreamy power loosened at the base of my spine
> and uncoiled and slid up through the marrow.
> A flow of seawater over the rock fell back
> with a she-hiss, plucking at my heel.
> My tongue stumbled ...

The sufficiency of conscious life, with its apparent understanding of experience, like the hypnotic flow of Kinsella's telling of what is happening, falters and we are forced into another kind of awareness:

> Who
>   is a breath
> that makes the wind
> that makes the wave
> that makes this voice?
>
> Who
>   is the bull with seven scars
> the hawk on the cliff
> the salmon sunk in his pool
> the pool sunk in her soil
> the animal's fury
> the flower's fibre
> a teardrop in the sun?

This mysterious unpredictable shift in perception, embodied in Kinsella's freeing of the poetic line, can be troubling to the reader who expects to have the experience at the poem's source formally proposed and conclusively reconciled. Similarly, Kinsella's structural shifts strain under the high-tension force of very diverse perceptual circumstances. In *A Technical Supplement*, the poem's structure is well-established in 24 sections, but the experiential core of the poem is too diffuse and uncentred. The language is, accordingly, often overstretched by a need to prove only its relevance to each of the parts:

> The point, greatly enlarged,
> pushed against the skin
> depressing an area of tissue.
> Rupture occurred: at first a separation
> at the intensest place among the cells
> then a deepening damage
> with nerve-strings fraying
> and snapping and writhing back.
> Blood welled up to fill the wound,
> bathing the point as it went deeper.
>
> Persist.

III

Song of the Night and Other Poems and *The Messenger* are much more balanced between each of their parts and the unified sequence. Not only are they placed within a discernible range of biographical, physical and cultural detail, but, unlike *A Technical Supplement*, their internal workings never obscure the reasons, objects, moods and feelings of the poems as a self-sustaining linguistic artifact in its own right.

Song of the Night and Other Poems is a captivating sequence from its opening image ("A stern moon-stare shed all over my brain/as he carried me, warm and chill,/homeward, abandoned, onward to the next shadow") to the close:

> The bay—every inlet—lifted
> and glittered toward us in articulated light.
> The land, a pitch-black stage
> of boulder shapes and scalps of heaped weed,
> inhaled.
>
> A part of the mass

grated and tore, cranking harshly,
and detached and struggled upward
and beat past us along the rocks,
bat-black, heron-slow.

Song of the Night, with its starkly articulate, prismatic self-consciousness and lunar-like landscapes, dramatises man's ecstatic isolation and sense of the world as spectacularly separate:

She was standing in a sheltered angle,
urgent and quiet.
'Look back ...'

The great theatre of Connemara,
dark. A cloud bank stretched in folds
across the sky, luminous
with inner activity.

Centred on the beached lamp
a single cell of cold light,
part land and part living water,
blazed with child voices.

The journey that underscores 'Song of Night' is a universal one, whether the focus is on Inistiogue or Philadelphia. Shadowed by the past (the "Black and Tan ghosts" as much as the "old immediacies" of love letters), *Song of the Night* defines an inner freedom from all its claims, as in the respite that work brings, of a nurse's song ('C.G. Jung's "First Years"') or "Overhead a curlew—God in Heaven!—... 'poignant ...'/Yes!/'hauntingly beautiful ...' Yes!'". Big words and elaborate phrases can appear as intrusions to the poems of *Song of the Night.* In *The Messenger,* however, Kinsella overlooks such issues and retells the relationship between two men—himself and his father.

It is intriguing to notice that these seemingly autobiographical poems of Kinsella's rarely tell us much about his own feelings. As Gabriel Pearson has said of Robert Lowell's poems: "The materials of his own life are there to be made over to art"[9] and it is *this* ordering of art that makes the Peppercanister poems such fascinating reading.

In *The Messenger,* not only do we get a substantial portrait of John Paul Kinsella as a man, but also what made him: the city he grew up in, his work, his aspirations, his death. *The Messenger* is a powerful piece of writing in its economical, mocking, fully focused refusal to elegise. The courage of an individual life, often easily misplaced in the customary rhetoric of 'A People', is finely adjudged in the following extract, as the young witnessing boy is recollected by the older poet at Mass with his father in the Oblate Fathers:

I made faces at my ghost in the brawn marble.
The round shaft went up shining
into a mouth of stone flowers

and the angry words echoed among
the hanging lamps, off the dark golden walls,
telling every Catholic how to vote.

He covered my hand with his
and we started getting out
in the middle of Mass past everybody.

Father Collier's top half in the pulpit
in a muscular black soutane and white lace
grabbed the crimson velvet ledge

—thick white hair, glasses,
a red face, a black mouth—
shouting Godless Russia at us.

The Joyce-like detail, the incontrovertible truthfulness of the scene as poetry (and vice versa), fix *The Messenger* not merely in a particular time and place, but give its very historicity an imaginative authority which is echoed later in 'Invocation' from *Songs of the Psyche*:

Judge not.
But judge.

Between the dramatised scene of *The Messenger* and the contradictory ambiguity of the 'Invocation' from *Songs of the Psyche*, Kinsella finds the specific imaginative root and tension for his poetry. It is this relationship, and the limits to which Kinsella is prepared to push it, that makes this poetry absolutely distinctive and incapable of imitation.

IV

One can speculate how Kinsella's influence on Irish poetry has been most pointed as an example, not solely in terms of artistic ambition, but, more profoundly, in terms of diction. He has flushed out the complacent poeticisms that obscure the language of poetry in Ireland by writing in an anti-eloquent diction, similar in effect to Montale's reaction against the excessively hermetic lyricism of Italian poetry. Like Montale, it is the tone of voice, as much as the settings and objects of his poetry, that sets Kinsella apart from his contemporaries.

G. Singh's remarks about the Italian poet's "dealing with what is rooted in personal experience and yet which is held out before us as something to be contemplated—as Montale himself contemplates it—with a certain degree of detachment and objectivity"[10] relates to this matter of tone and its place in poetry in the English language. One looks, for instance, at the grin of despair in Philip Larkin, the muscular rage of Derek Walcott, Joseph Brodsky's sublimities, Geoffrey Hill's high austerity, but without finding an appropriate context for Kinsella. Placing him alongside other Irish poets is equally unsatisfactory—Kavanagh, Montague, Heaney, Mahon ...?

There does not seem to be an acceptable poetic context for Kinsella, Irish or otherwise, except perhaps if one considers Lowell or goes back a little to a poet like Montale or the Greek poet George Seferis. For in Montale and Seferis, one discovers a European setting profoundly engrained with a national culture (Italian or Greek), torn by political division (civil war), but dependent upon a deeply *personal* and self-analytical imagination, conscious all the time that, in the making of art, a poet stands out and up against the ignomies of history. This awareness is both a good and bad thing.

On the negative side, it can lead to a ponderous, inclusive abstraction that denies to poetry its song and music; on the positive side, it means that a poet cannot become complacent because of an inherited disturbance at the heart of his culture which disrupts the poise of the writing, underpinning it with an unmistakable and unfakable realism. Kinsella's poetry contains both these impulses.

The realism of which I speak is not the documentary kind, of reportage and staying close to the nuances of a particular dialect or style of speech, although it can absorb these. From *New Poems* onwards, Kinsella's poetry broke into the structure of language itself.

How do we articulate the past and what we see around us 'now'? What has brought us 'here' in the first place? What our family 'means' and how we gather all such 'things' into our 'selves'? These issues are questions at the very heart of Kinsella's poetry.

Kinsella also refuses to take anything as given. Consequently, the characteristic mood of his work is interrogative. The past features a good deal in the Peppercanister poems and he often seeks to reject its inevitable, consuming demands while, paradoxically, wanting to preserve it. Thus the other side of Kinsella's accomplishment, from his translation of *The Táin* (1969), *An Duanaire* (1981) with Seán O Tuama, and his edition of the *New Oxford Book of Irish Verse* (1986).

The guiding voice has consistently been cut through by clashing, unsettling images as the imagination registers reality. This simultaneous movement of Kinsella's poems breaches the normal, expected poetic narrative. The poet takes in what is significant to him, without forcing the issue into a necessary coherence; the focus resides in the imagination's ordering of reality. We either trust this, or the poem falls by the wayside.

V

In *Blood and Family*, Kinsella reserves this poetic right most persuasively. *Songs of the Psyche* deals with his own life and *Her Vertical Smile* portrays the figure of the artist with the haunted presence of Gustav Mahler. The opening scenes of *Songs of the Psyche* carry an immanently naturalistic power, reminiscent of the Joyce of *Dubliners*:

I took the grey animal book
from under the clothes in the drawer
and opened it at the Capuchin monkeys
in their forest home.

I asked Tom Ryan once: 'Tell me the print!'
but he only grinned and said
'I will if you can spell Wednesday'.
With his slithery walk ...

They were lighting the lamps
outside the shop and she started shouting:
'What are you up to in there?
Always stuck in that old room.'

There is a sense in which the poems of *Blood and Family* are themselves "stuck in that old room" of the past, with Kinsella, like Nathaniel Hawthorne, rummaging through the lumber of his people's history in the family house. The celebration, though, of the human spirit with which Kinsella associates Mahler in 'Her Vertical Smile', casts a wry smile over the great pursuit:

Nine are the enabling elements
    in the higher crafts
and the greatest of these is Luck.

I lift my
    baton and my
trousers fall.

In *Out of Ireland* and *St. Catherine's Clock*, Kinsella unpicks the familial and intellectual locks of his coiled and unclaimed inheritance, Irish and European. There stands, for instance, the figure of John Scotus Eriugena, the ninth-century Irish philosopher, and the sense of buried permanence that runs from him towards the present, on "the day we all came down from Cork/to commemorate our musical friend", Seán O Riada, in an ancient church. Both Scotus and O Riada embody an harmonious certainty; a creative resource of possibility:

            ... that the world's parts
ill-fitted in their stresses and their pains,
will combine at last in polyphonic sweet-breathing union
and all created Natures ascend ...

... stunned at the world's edge
silent in a choir of understanding.

As *Out of Ireland* literally moves in and out of this reconciliation, the poet recalls Eriugena's ideas and the occasion for his own reverie while "the staling music of memory" draws him back, inevitably, to what is real and actual. The medieval past and the present merge "with suspended understanding" as he leaves the ground of the church with its "grotesque head in the tower wall and a *sheela-na-gig*—an obscene cult or fertility figure—displayed in a depression above a window in the South wall"[11]:

A careful step

together over that outstuck
tongue, and shut this gate
in God's name

behind us, once and for all.
And reach me my weapon
in the goat-grey light.

The questionable sense of release that closes *Out of Ireland* is brought up short against the opening lines of *St. Catherine's Clock*:

The whole terrace
slammed shut.
I inhaled the granite lamplight,
divining the energies of the prowler.

St. Catherine's Clock is kept in this eerie half-light, as Kinsella homes in on a forgotten world, as submerged and unknown in its own way as the intellectual veracity of a Scotus Eriugena. For *St. Catherine's Clock* depicts the Dublin of political struggle and the ghastly cost, like Robert Emmet's execution:

The pasty head is separated and brandished aloft,
the dead forehead with the black wet lock
turned toward the Fountain.

The unrhetorical grim flourish here is related to other scenes of 18th-century urban life—the "pair of children or dwarfs,/a man and women with buckets,/a couple of mongrels/worrying the genitals out of each other"; "barefoot,/bowed in aged rags to the earth,/a hag/toils across the street"—and throughout *St. Catherine's Clock* the poet's imagination re-enacts the past as a form of repossession. Lodged firmly in the centre of this drama, that it may never get out of hand, is the unimpressed young lad:

... inside in the back room
up on the bed with a rolled-up newspaper
at the holy picture, killing flies.

Surrounding him are the ghost-lives, repressed, lived under toil, while the seemingly unbridgeable gulf between them and their own political and cultural inheritances defines the subject of estrangement and loss which binds together the Peppercanister poems. Exemplary and uncompromising as they may well be, these poems are confirmed by Thomas Kinsella's austere and ironic fidelity:

> And I always remembered
> who and what I am.

This assertive and determined commitment to "who and what" he is (and, by implication, artistically stands for) can hardly be an easy option, given the critical practice and assumptions which dominate discussion of Irish poetry. Thomas Kinsella may well have turned his face against the current of public acknowledgement and esteem that is now offered to Irish poets in their own country but also in Britain and elsewhere. Yet the recognition he deserves is of a different order, since Kinsella's vision of 'blood and family' threads its own difficult path through the modern Irish labyrinth, without fear or favour.

Notes

[1] Quotations from Thomas Kinsella's poetry are taken from: *Poems 1956-1973* (Mountrath: Dolmen Press, 1980), *Peppercanister Poems 1972-1978* (North Carolina: Wake Forest University Press, 1979), *Blood and Family* (Oxford: Oxford University Press, 1988).

[2] *Viewpoints: Poets in Conversation with John Haffenden* (London: Faber & Faber, 1981), p. 103.

[3] ibid., p. 104.

[4] 'Time and the Poet', Appendix III in Caroline A. Rosenberg *Let Our Gaze Blaze: The Recent Poetry of Thomas Kinsella* (Ann Arbor Michigan/London University Microfilms International 1982), p. 103.

[5] *Viewpoints*, pp. 102-103.

[6] 'Poetry since Yeats: An Exchange of Views', *Tri-Quarterly* (No. 4, 1965) p. 106.

[7] ibid., p. 106.

[8] *Viewpoints*, p. 104.

[9] Quoted in Ian Hamilton, *Robert Lowell: A Biography* (London, Faber & Faber, 1983), p. 105.

[10] G. Singh, 'Introduction' to *Montale: Selected Poems* (Manchester: Manchester University Press, 1975), p. 13.

[11] In an author's note to *Out of Ireland*.

9

Invocation of Powers

John Montague

I

In the title essay of his collection, *The Figure in the Cave and other Essays*[1], John Montague reveals the extent to which his adult life and work have been directed towards creating for himself a central place in the Irish literary canon. It is an ambition, as the essay outlines, deeply influenced by the experiences Montague underwent as a child, first uprooted from his family in New York, and subsequently returned to Northern Ireland as a foster-child in the care of elderly aunts in County Tyrone. The sense of dislocation that pervades Montague's poetry, and the self-conscious search for both a real (emotional) and imagined (cultural) home, represent the twin matters which I want to discuss. What the bond between these two preoccupations proves to be in John Montague's poetry is the presentation of his own 'self' as it responds to, and anticipates, various elements in Irish literary and political history.

The essay to which I have referred is important in this particular regard for, as the editor of his essays, Antoinette Quinn, has pointed out, Montague is "primarily an autobiographical poet for whom the provincial and local unrest and violence, whether historical or contemporary, are extensions of ancestral, familial and personal traumas".[2]

In 'The Figure in the Cave', Montague relates his personal life-story to his artistic life. At several points, they intersect and are made to take on an historical significance of self-mythologising:

> ... Brooklyn-born, Tyrone-reared, Dublin-educated, constituted a tangle, a turmoil of contradictory allegiance it would take a lifetime to unravel. And the chaos within contrasted with the false calm without: Ireland, both North and South, then seemed to me 'a fen of stagnant waters'. And there was no tradition for someone of my background to work in; except for the ahistorical genius of Kavanagh, just across the border, there had not been a poet of Ulster Catholic background since the Gaelic poets of the eighteenth century. So when I describe myself as 'the missing link of Ulster poetry' I am not only joking, for, hard as it may be to understand today, there was no Northern dimension to Irish literature then ...

The "then" is the late 50s and early 60s. What Montague is clearly seeking to establish here is his own place in Irish literature, notwithstanding the "ahistorical genius of Kavanagh". Throughout the essay, Montague informs us of the role he played in restoring to print such poets as John Hewitt and Patrick Kavanagh[4]; how he simultaneously promoted the notion of what he calls "the French idea of a fertile literary community" since he "would not wish anyone to go through what [he] endured as a young writer". Montague goes on to list his work in this regard: *The Dolmen Miscellany of Irish Writing* (1961), *The Faber Book of Irish Verse* (1974) and *Bitter Harvest* (1989).[5]

Having therefore outlined his making available a tradition that was either historical (the Gaelic poets of the 18th century) or otherwise obscured (like Kavanagh or Hewitt), Montague traces the wider net of his ambition by revealing his "veneration for older writers of genius", such as Ezra Pound, Wallace Stevens, Hugh MacDiarmid, Robert Graves, David Jones, Samuel Beckett and Austin Clarke:

> Graves was also writing in a tradition of love poetry going back to the *amour courtois* which began ... in the valley of the Dordogne, a tradition in which I also inscribe myself, with modern hesitations. But I was always fond of my literary fathers, in verse and prose, and they usually returned the compliment.[6]

As earlier in the essay, when Montague writes of his own name and its changing from Tague to Montague ("I have played upon our change of name and am delighted that in the original Irish *taidgh* means 'son of the philosopher, poet or fool': I claim all three")[7], so too in the above extract the important point of note for present purposes is the identification with other writers as "my literary fathers" and the implicit sense of approval-seeking. This form of self-vindication is furthered by the preoccupied manner in which Montague relates himself to "several interlocking groups of writers" outside Ireland, from Gary Snyder, Robert Duncan, Charles Tomlinson and Ted Hughes, to poets writing in languages other than English, such as Octavio Paz. The tradition-making, which such listing implies, bears down directly upon one of the concluding motifs from 'The Figure in the Cave' as essay and as collection.

For Montague meditates on the way "destiny seems to have decided to give me back my lost childhood in America" with the honour of a first US honorary doctorate and a reception from both houses of the New York legislature while "my Tyrone background is being destroyed by bulldozer and bomb. Ballygawley is now as black a name as the South Bronx or Brooklyn";

> It is like a fairytale, the little child who was sent away being received back with open arms. But while awed at the reappearance of this golden cradle to rock my dotage, I am grateful to have explored Ireland so intimately. Standing-stones and streams are not part of Brooklyn nor are *cailleachs.* To judge by my contemporaries I would probably have been a writer, certainly a journalist, had I stayed in America. But who cut the long wound of poetry into my youth? Was it my mother who chose for her own good reasons to cast me off? [8]

II

John Montague has published ten collections of poetry between *Forms of Exile* (1958) and *Mount Eagle* (1988). Alongside these volumes, two works of fiction have appeared: *Death of a Chieftain* (1964) and *The Lost Notebook* (1988). It would be impractical to deal with Montague's work in its entirety, including the editorial and critical writing, so I intend to focus instead upon a cluster of poems which act as an imaginative counterweight to my introduction.

It will be recalled that, in the last quotation from 'The Figure in the Cave', Montague directly associated poetry with "the long wound" and his sense of being "cast off". Poetry is both an affliction and, by implication, a mode of consolation and compensation. The individual 'self' is repatriated to the lost homeland through poetry and held up as a focus of (predominantly inherited) social, political, literary and cultural experiences. The overriding impression this figure presents in Montague's poetry is that of a 'victim'.

There are, for instance, the portraits of womanhood such as the *cailleach* (Ir. old woman, hag), from 'The Wild Dog Rose'[9], who suffers rape and loneliness; the "old bitch, with a warm mouthful of game" in 'Dowager'[10], representative of the Anglo-Irish caste, humming "with satisfaction in the sun". More convincingly, there is Nurse Mullen from 'Herbert Street Revisited'[11], who "knelt by her bedside/to pray for her lost Mayo hills,/the bruised bodies of Easter Volunteers" before her own death, "upright/in her chair, facing a window/warm with the blue slopes of Nephin".

The characteristic gesture is passive acceptance: "treading the pattern/of one time and place into history" as Montague remarks in 'Herbert Street Revisited'. Resignation or acceptance is a typical note in the poetry as memories are fixed upon family items like a locket or a silver flask.[12] In the face of Nature, too, the dominant note is elegiac; the landscape representing "a manuscript/We had lost the skill to read,/A part of our past disinherited".[13]

The landscape becomes impregnated with historical signs and symbols which the poet decodes as best he can, knowing, all the while, of the "severed head" which "chokes to/speak another tongue":

To slur and stumble

        In shame
the altered syllables
of your own name;
to stray sadly home

        And find
the turf cured width
of your parent's hearth
growing slowly alien
...
        To grow
a second tongue, as
harsh a humiliation
as twice to be born.

        Decades later
that child's grandchild's
speech stumbles over lost
syllables of an old order.[14]

From figures of the victim, to a sense of resignation and the very "humiliation" of finding his ancestral language suppressed, the poet seeks an understanding of his own 'speech' in 'The Sound of a Wound':

> Scar tissue
> can rend, the old hurt
> tear open as
> the torso of the fiddle
> groans to
> carry the tune, to carry
> the pain of
> a lost (slow herds of cattle
> roving over
> soft meadow, dark bogland)
> pastoral rhythm.[15]

Yet out of this loss, "the old hurt", Montague summons, "in my bloodstream", bitterness inherited

> ... from my father, the
> swarm of blood
> to the brain, the vomit surge
> of race hatred,
> the victim seeing the oppressor,
> bold Jacobean
> planter, or gadget laden marine,
> who has scatter-
> ed his household gods, used
> his people
> as servants, flushed his women
> like game.

The recurrence of this image of the wound and its association with loss is unmistakable in Montague's poetry. His father, "a traditional Irishman" in 'The Cage'[16], is reimagined: "his bald head behind/the bars of the small booth;/the mark of an old car/accident beating on his/ghostly forehead", while in the uncollected poem, 'Sands', about the IRA hunger-striker who died, the reconciliation of wound as metaphor with loss is subsumed into the absolute mark of sacrifice as an historical birthright:

This is a sign of silence.
This is the sound of the bone
breaking through skin
of a slowly wasting man.
This is the sound of his death:
but also of his living on.[17]

This is quite close in tone to the famous rhetoric of Patrick Pearse and his vision of sacrifice, a belief that sustained the hunger-strikers in the 80s as much as beforehand: the rhetoric which other Irish writers, like O'Casey, have questioned and exposed. Indeed, discussing this very point in relation to Irish drama, Philip Edwards commented upon "the intoxicating power of the language of romantic nationalism, a *damnosa hereditas*, that cannot be shaken off. If modern Irish drama is a drama of victims, they are chiefly victims of language".[18] In this way, too, Montague is making poetry from the assimilation of the 'victim' with language and his own recreated sense of his 'self' as constituted by these same forces.

As Nadine Gordimer has remarked in another context, "There is no moral authority like that of sacrifice".[19] This has obviously influenced, to put it at its mildest, the critical and historical terms of reference (and expectation) by which much, if not all, of Irish poetry has been received by readers and critics alike, particularly in the United States but also in Britain and Ireland. The important point to stress is that Montague's role in establishing these terms, both imaginatively and critically, anticipates[20] the poetic negotiations a writer such as Seamus Heaney was to make in, for example, *Wintering Out* (1973) and *North* (1975).

In his early experiences as an 'exile' of sorts, who returns on a voyage of rediscovery, his country origins framed by the coloniser's tongue, in a political state not of his or his family's making or choosing, Montague *represents* an identifiable pattern in his life and art. One consolidates the other in recognisable, even predictable, ways, so that the creative triangle (poetry as wound, victim of language, and the *inherited* sense of self seen as essential characteristics of Irish literature and history) forms an almost archetypal mandatory ritual, irresistible in its appeal to writer and audience alike:

Grounded for the second time
my tongue became a rusted hinge

until the sweet oils of poetry

eased it and light flooded in.[21]

In the background of Montague's poetry, there is that much-quoted passage from Joyce's *A Portrait of the Artist as a Young Man* when, facing the Dean of Studies, Stephen thinks:

> —The language in which we are speaking is his before it is mine. How different are the words *home, Christ, ale, master*, on his lips and on mine! I cannot speak or write these words without unrest of spirit. His language, so familiar and so foreign, will always be for me an acquired speech. I have not made or accepted its words. My voice holds them a bay. My soul frets in the shadow of his language.[22]

The 70 and more years which separate Joyce's fictional character and Joyce's own obsessive and unique relationship with the English language can still aesthetically sustain a poet like Montague, and one need only turn to Seamus Heaney's *Station Island* (1984) for further illustration of this resilient theme. So dominant is it in effect that, unlike the Big House/Ascendancy motif in Irish writing, little discussion has taken place as to how relevant Stephen Dedalus's words actually are *now* to Irish experience and the social and political realities of the island, notwithstanding the powerful universal appeal of Joyce's story.

III

In John Bayley's *The Uses of Division*, the chapter which deals with the poetry of John Berryman, Robert Lowell and Philip Larkin, contains the following remark:

> The public status and recognition of poets in Russia, in the smaller European countries or in Spanish America, puts them in a different class: to be a national poetic rhetorician, like Mayakovsky or Neruda, is to be in some sense naïve, to achieve power through naïveté. And not to be *taken in*, not to be thus socially and nationally innocent, is vital to the working of the poetry we are discussing.[23]

The section of the chapter from which this quotation comes is called 'The Self as Available Reality' (after R.P. Blackmur) and it represents the kind of tension that characterises the poetry of John Montague. For his work is caught between two poles of attraction: the 'national poetic rhetoric' and 'naïveté' of an acquired outrage and bitterness, as exhibited in *The Rough Field,* ranged against the later Lowellesque self-dramatisations of *The Dead Kingdom.* As Bayley remarks in the second section, 'The Importance of Elsewhere':

> ... it is difficult not to conclude that the dynamic of today's [1976] best poetry is a setting up in it of the poet, which, when accomplished, constitutes an aesthetic goal. The poet has arrived in our midst, his newness defined by the personal reality of the self his art has brought to us.[24]

In Montague, the aesthetic goal is the personal reality, of making an imaginative home for himself out of a powerful, monolithic and conservative literary and cultural tradition. This means that, like a divining rod, his imagination wavers from the assembled sequences of love lyrics and recollection in *The Great Cloak* and *The Dead Kingdom* to the epical aspiration of attempting a poetry that will be shaped through (and in turn shape?) an entire province's history, torn by moral, political and cultural division, such as he finds in the north of Ireland:

> Lines of leaving
>   lines of returning
> the long estuary
>   of Lough Foyle, a
> ship motionless
>   in wet darkness
> mournfully hooting
>   as a tender creeps
> to carry passengers
>   back to Ireland
> a child of four
>   this sad sea city
> my landing place
>   the loneliness of
> Lir's white daughter's
>   ice crusted wings
> forever spread
>   at the harbour mouth.[25]

Personal reality here assumes historical proportions and vice versa. The poet inherits the past *a priori* and the poetry conveys, again compliantly, an already given identity for the self: "a child of four/ this sad sea city/my landing place."

Ironically, perhaps, when glossing this poem, Montague seemed to be advocating "a deliberate programme of denationalisation", but went on to say that "all true experiments and exchanges only serve to illuminate the self, a rediscovery of the oldest laws of the psyche".[26] Yet it is true to say that much of Montague's own poetry is bound up with the nation-place and nationalism, with what he has called "our racial drama of conscience".[27] Irish mythology, such as Lir's daughters, is never far from the surface and many of his poems deal with Irish cultural icons; for example, the Irish landscape or the 'loss' of the Irish language. Furthermore, an elegy like 'O Riada's Farewell'— "pride of music/pride of race"—concerning the premature death of the musician and composer Seán O Riada, carries an almost talismanic significance in recent Irish poetry.[28] It is in this poem that one sees clearly enough Montague's intention of restoring to life what he had earlier called, in 'The Road's End', the "shards/of a lost culture"[29] since 'O Riada's Farewell' hears Ezra Pound's flourish, "To have gathered from the air a live tradition".[30] The poem provides us with a useful text in more ways than one since it shows how, in the characteristic gesture of a lament, memorialising the past and life of one man goes beyond the celebration of the solely human:

> And a nation mourns:
> The blind horseman with his harp carrying servant,
> Hurrying through darkness to a great house
> Where a lordly welcome waits, as here:
>
> Fingernail spikes in candlelight recall
> A ripple & rush of upland streams,
> The slant of rain on void eye sockets,
> The shrill of snipe over mountains
> Where a few stragglers nest in bracken—
> After Kinsale, after Limerick, after Aughrim,
> After another defeat, to be redeemed
> By the curlew sorrow of an aisling.[31]

What is more, the poem itself is an act of redeeming what has gone or been lost: for 'defeat' read 'aisling'; the imagination lodged in the heroic past converts its failures (Kinsale, Limerick, Aughrim) to compensatory images of acceptance, the "curlew sorrow" of the impoverished present. However, this process, of "a lost pastoral rhythm", begs a central question of Montague's own imaginative priorities and the extent to which he has created, in John Bayley's words, "supreme beauty out of ugliness, emptiness and contingency, the trapped and the doomed ... (while keeping) us continuously interested in himself, always wanting to hear more about him". This is the real aesthetic risk a prolific autobiographical poet such as John Montague takes, given as well the cultural agenda he has set for himself:

> *Dia dhuit/*
> *Dia agus Muire dhuit/*
> *Dia agus Muire*
> *agus Padraig dhuit*
> invocation of powers
> to cleanse the mind.
> Then the question
> and answer.
> 'What did she say?'
> I was asked when I came back to the car
> but could only point the way
> over the hill to where
> obscured in sea
> mist, the small, grey stones of the oratory
> held in the Atlantic for a thousand years.[32]

IV

It is the "thousand years" which stands as a metaphorical locus for most of John Montague's poetry; the ancestral haunting of the present as much as the present obscuring the past.[33] Montague attempts to embody this duality, and the most revealing aspect of his work is its sense of foreboding, an anticipation of closure and completion. For his poems deal in half-light, dawns or dusks, elusive moments of recollection, when the frisson of political or sexual tension has passed and the poet draws attention to their significance. This narrative urge to resolve his poems can falter, however, and lead into the clichéd rhetoric of, for instance, his poem in memory of Hugh MacDiarmid, 'Scotia', from *Mount Eagle*:

Nourishing a lonely dream of how
this desolate country might have been!
The rightful arrogance of MacDiarmid's
calling together of Clann Albann,
or the surging lamentations of MacLean,
the sound of his echoing Gaelic
a fierce pibroch crying on the wind.[34]

Whereas in 'Discords', also from *Mount Eagle*, the rhetorical question that closes the first section of the poem carries a personally charged vindication clearly absent from the ceremonial poems such as 'Scotia':

There is a white light in the room.
It is anger. He is angry, or
She is angry, or both are angry.
To them it is absolute, total,
It is everything: but to the visitor,
The onlooker, the outsider,
It is the usual, the absurd;
For if they did not love each other
Why should they heed a single word?[35]

These two persistent directions of Montague's writing—one autobiographical, the other explicitly cultural—can find themselves insufficiently sustained by a distinct imaginative *raison d'être*. This lack means that some of Montague's poetry has a conventional air of being written to a prefabricated formula, with certain stock images and characters guaranteeing the 'Irish' authenticity of his work.[36] This may be linked to an awareness of what Stephen Spender outlined in the introduction to his study of Anglo-American sensibilities, *Love-Hate Relations*.

When describing the contrasting attractions of the American writer for Europe (and England) as against the establishing of a 'native' literature (Williams *v.* Eliot), Spender comments on the "connection between their separate existence [autobiography] and their country, in its history, landscape and people". He goes on:

This awareness is of a life which is that of an ideal United States or England which the writer, if he is in a correct relation to it, relates in his work. Unless he does have such a relation, his work will be peripheral to the centre or turned inward on himself. It follows that if the nation itself

> presents conditions which prevent the writer identifying it with the ideal of the country of the mind, then he will find himself opposed to the official nation. His work will find its centre in a patriotism against which he measures the surrounding public nation. To simplify my argument let me call the idea of a true nation, 'the patria'.[37]

In Ireland, the modern 'idea of a nation' has of course been efficiently repossessed and institutionalised by the political course of nationalism and poets were (*are*?) generally seen as guardians of that sacred[38], rather than civic, duty. There are many questions at issue here, too many to be discussed in an essay such as the present one. One thinks, for example, of the complicated relationship between 'old' and 'new' cultures and of how, paradoxically, a *nation* like Ireland's is both simultaneously. There is also the sense in which 'the patria' in Spender's terms can be viewed autobiographically as the individual's generalised search for a father-figure; the nation, his or her home; the idealised community, the family. Or, more specifically, the manner in which a poet like John Montague sees himself self-consciously as a bridge between these divides of American, European and Irish cultures in his own life and through his own writing. Thus, when he states the following in 'The Impact of International Modern Poetry on Irish Writing' (1973), one senses the ground being cleared for his own role:

> The only literary art in which we have not made our presence felt is the one in which we are supposed to excel: this is, poetry. Yeats apart, few Irish poets have been accepted as international figures in the way that Pablo Neruda is, or Octavio Paz, or Ungaretti.[39]

The essential point I take from Stephen Spender's introduction concerns 'patria', the national ground out of which "international figures" emerge, set alongside the "ideal United States or England [or Ireland] which the writer, if he is in correct relation to it, releases in his work". Whatever qualifications one may have about that phrase "correct relation", the ideal Ireland that has been released in John Montague's poetry is effectively *now* the official version. One can go a step further and even suggest that a possible reading of Montague's poetry is that it completes and concludes the cultural (and I stress, *cultural*) agenda Yeats set down by redefining that movement of Irish literary nationalism from a northern republican point of view. For, at various stages, Montague has insisted upon the non-English but 'European' dimension of Irish literature. His comments on exile in 'The Impact of International Modern Poetry on Irish Writing' are a case in point, as are his remarks on Louis MacNeice whose work Montague sees "very much in the non-experimental tradition of English modern poetry, and, as such, nearly unexportable".[40]

Matters of trade apart, somewhat later in the same broadcast, when describing the poetry of Denis Devlin and Austin Clarke in terms of "our racial drama of conscience", Montague proclaims that while "difficult to define (perhaps because the imperial habit dies hard, and the British Council is a more subtle version of the *Pax Britannica*) an Irish writer has a better chance of being a European than has an Englishman".[41] Yet such potentiality is qualified in Montague's mind by the injunction that "if one is going to be influenced by contemporary poetry outside Ireland, it should be at first hand and not by hearsay, years after the event".[42]

The imperative sense here of the contemporaneity of poetry and the necessarily *positive* value of 'influences' *per se* are recalled in Montague's follow-on comment to the effect that having "participated in one of the early readings of *Howl*, I found it depressing when the Ginsberg wave broke over Ireland a decade later, drowning many potential young poets".[43]

The subjective reading assumes an impersonal critical status, yet who these "young poets" were is left out of the account. They represent an audience of failure somewhat remote ('hearsay') from where the poet himself is—at the heart of things: "we move in a world which is increasingly both local *and* international, and in poetry, as in science, there is nothing so irrelevant as repeating someone else's experiments."[44]

Montague includes in his talk an admonition of the "majority of Irish poets" who write "as though Pound, Lawrence, Williams, had not brought a new music into English poetry, as though the iambic line still registered the curve of modern speech".[45] Against this 'majority' failure on most sides, Montague requests, in a characteristic flourish, that "an Irish poet should be familiar with the finest work of his contemporaries, not just the increasingly narrow English version of modern poetry, or the more extensive American one, but in other languages as well". He goes on:

> I would say that my contemporaries are not just the Irish poets I admire, but those with whom I feel an affinity elsewhere, Ponge in France, Octavio Paz in Mexico, Gary Snyder and Robert Duncan in San Francisco. I seem to be advocating a deliberate programme of de-nationalisation, but all true experiments and exchanges only serve to illuminate the self, a rediscovery of the oldest laws of the psyche.[46]

So we are back at that intersection of "a thousand years", with the added presence of nominated international figures at the crossroads. It is important to remind ourselves of the date of this broadcast—1973—and of how it was in the late 60s and early 70s that other voices, indisputably Irish in experience and accent, confidently familiar with developments in European and American poetry and trained in English literature, were establishing themselves in the forefront of the public mind and critical press. Names like Seamus Heaney, Derek Mahon, Seamus Deane and Michael Longley. Freed from any need to prove themselves or the ground of their being poets (northern or otherwise), they moved with self-determination, absorbing in the main the artistic legacy of W.B. Yeats, rather than the left-overs of his cultural programme, such as it was.

'Denationalisation' as applied to the poetry of any one of these poets sounds incongruous and out of place and as dated as Montague's exhortation that his fellow Irish poets must look beyond their own immediate borders. Such transcendence is imaginatively assumed in the work of these other poets and is also one of the central intellectual preoccupations in the critical writings of Seamus Heaney and Seamus Deane.[47]

In this sense, John Montague has been vindicated by the example of his younger peers whose very difference challenges any deterministic or inherited formulation of what a poet should or should not do, read or write about. The only exigency is the recognition of individual talent and the limits of tradition.

There is the unimpeachable wisdom of Philip Larkin's comment to bear in mind in this regard. When responding to a request from D.J. Enright for a brief statement of his views on poetry, Larkin replied:

> I find it hard to give any abstract views on poetry and its present condition as I find theorising on the subject no help to me as a writer. In fact it would be true to say that I make a point of not knowing what poetry is or how to

> read a page or about the function of myth. It is fatal to decide, intellectually, what good poetry is because you are then in honour bound to try to write it, instead of the poems that only you can write.[48]

It is an early example (1955) of Larkin-speak, deceitfully sharp-witted *and* intuitive, preserving the private, almost secretive sources of his own imagination, and bluntly refusing to budge or reveal anything of himself. With certain changes in register, this could be Cavafy speaking, but the stabilising force and composure of the English tradition in poetry acts like a rudder behind the concluding phrase, "the poems that only you can write". For the sense of who 'you' are as a writer strikes me as being one of, if not *the*, most important themes in John Montague's writing. His poetry and criticism (and fiction, for that matter) believe in the rhetorical weight of showing what *should* be done, read, claimed, written about, in order that a local field, like Garvaghey, can enjoy as much imaginative light as will also illuminate the amenable profiles of one's self. This is the insistently moral ambience of Montague's work which sees the autobiographical and cultural as one and the same recurrent imaginative project: the poet as oracle, invoker of powers. In this regard, Montague is very much more a traditionalist than he would have us believe from his comments on experimentalism, international writing and so forth. His poetry is lodged firmly in the custodianship of generous images of good[49], rather than in the quicksand of a modernism either fiercely introverted or aggressively peripheral.[50]

In establishing, or re-establishing, this ancient territorial rite, Montague probably made it possible for a poet like Seamus Heaney to speak out of his own experience without loss of face, or, for that matter, of faith in the mythic possibilities of poetry.

Yet throughout Montague's poetry there is a stylisation of experience which is essentially literary; and that works against its epic grain. It is as if the poet were self-consciously setting out to prove something—about his past and its potency as a poetic theme. This side to Montague's poetry is characteristic of quite a lot of Irish writing in the 70s and 80s. As critics rarely fail to remind us, it has a direct bearing upon the colonised basis of English as a language spoken and written in Ireland. Certainly, the bardic strain associated with the tradition of Irish poetry in Gaelic breaks through Montague's poems and reveals a world strangely subsumed in the highly polished and achieved form of its expression, as in some of Montague's best-known lyrics—'The Wild Dog Rose', 'The Sean Bhean Bocht' and 'A Lost Tradition'.

John Montague stands as the epitome of that dominant view of Irish poetry which derives from the national ideas, heritage and messianic ideals forged as the cultural foundation of the Irish state[51] and rehearsed in the mind and experience of one of its prodigal sons. He sees his work strictly and reverentially as the sexual, political and cultural communion of his life with its natural homeland, the creation of an internationally recognisable identity called 'Irish Poet'.

Notes

[1] John Montague, *The Figure in the Cave and other Essays* (Dublin: The Lilliput Press, 1989).

[2] Antoinette Quinn, 'The Well-Beloved': Montague and the Muse', in *Irish University Review* (Vol. 19, No. 1, Spring 1989). Ms. Quinn's essay elaborates upon these themes and in particular, Montague's sense of being "a virtual orphan ... continually seeking to compensate for the maternal bonding of which he was deprived in infancy". The present writer will not pursue the psychological dimensions of such a quest, but rather concentrate upon the nature of their transformation into art.

[3] *The Figure in the Cave*, pp. 8-9. The blurb on the cover of Montague's *Mount Eagle* (Meath: The Gallery Press, 1988) states: "John Montague commands a pivotal place in contemporary Irish writing. His achievement ... may be seen as a vital link between Patrick Kavanagh's instruction and a number of important younger poets."

[4] *The Figure in the Cave*, p. 10 "I was editing the poetry of Patrick Kavanagh in the background ..."; "In helping to get Kavanagh and Hewitt back into print" p. 15.

[5] ibid., p. 15.

[6] ibid., It is interesting to note Montague's 'Introduction' to *Poisoned Lands* (new ed. Dublin: Dolmen Press, 1977): "An editor-poet I studiously avoided was T.S. Eliot but, when the volume was being considered for American publication, it crossed his desk. Old Possum risked a friendly pat: 'I have, indeed, found Mr. Montague's poems worthy of study'", p. 10.

[7] *The Figure in the Cave*, p. 11.

[8] ibid., pp. 17-18.

[9] *The Rough Field* (Meath: The Gallery Press, 1989), pp. 78-80.

[10] *A Slow Dance* (Dublin: Dolmen Press, 1975), p. 23.

[11] *The Great Cloak* (Dublin: Dolmen Press, 1978), pp. 40-42.

[12] 'The Locket' and 'The Silver Flask' in *The Dead Kingdom* (Mountrath: Dolmen Press, 1984), p. 92,72.

[13] *The Rough Field*, p. 35.

[14] ibid., p. 39.
[15] ibid, pp. 44-45.
[16] ibid., p. 46. Entitled 'Cage', but subsequently reprinted in *Selected Poems* (London: Oxford University Press, 1982) and *New Selected Poems* (Meath: The Gallery Press, 1989) as 'The Cage'.
[17] *Aquarius* (15/16, 1983/84), p. 80.
[18] Philip Edwards, *Threshold of a Nation: A Study in English and Irish Drama* (Cambridge: Cambridge University Press, 1979), p. 232.
[19] Nadine Gordimer, *The Essential Gesture: Writing, Politics and Places* (London: Jonathan Cape,1988), p. 294.
[20] Montague says as much himself in 'Dennis O'Driscoll: An Interview with John Montague', *Irish University Review*, Vol. 19, No. 1 (Spring 1989), "... I ante-date this new emphasis on Ulster writing. I mean I had done *Poisoned Lands, Death of a Chieftain* and I was working on *The Rough Field.* I have described myself as the missing link of Ulster poetry", p. 60.
[21] John Montague, 'A Flowering Absence', *The Dead Kingdom*, p. 91.
[22] James Joyce, *A Portrait of the Artist as a Young Man* (London: Jonathan Cape, 1920), p. 215.
[23] John Bayley, *The Uses of Division: Unity & Disharmony in Literature* (London: Chatto & Windus, 1976), p. 165.
[24] ibid., p. 177.
[25] *The Rough Field*, p. 73.
[26] 'The Impact of International Modern Poetry on Irish Writing', *The Figure in the Cave and other Essays*, p. 219.
[27] ibid., p. 213.
[28] *cf.* Thomas Kinsella, 'A Selected Life & Vertical Man', *Fifteen Dead* (Dublin: Dolmen Press, 1979); Seamus Heaney, 'In Memorium Seán O Riada', *Field Work* (London: Faber and Faber, 1979) and Seán Lucy, '*Unfinished Sequence* for Seán O Riada', *Unfinished Sequence* (Dublin: Wolfhound Press, 1979).
[29] *A Chosen Light* (London: MacGibbon & Kee, 1967), p. 32.
[30] *A Slow Dance*, p. 57.
[31] ibid., p. 62.
[32] *A Chosen Light*, p. 37.
[33] Thus the three-faced stone-head (c. 3rd-2nd B.C.) that adorns the cover of *New Selected Poems* (1989).
[34] *Mount Eagle*, p. 61.
[35] ibid., p. 45.
[36] *cf.* Richard J. Loftus, *Nationalism in Modern Anglo-Irish Poetry* (Madison and Milwaukee: University of Wisconsin Press, 1964), pp. 16-17. One of the more critical readings of modern Irish poetry available.
[37] Stephen Spender, *Love-Hate Relations: A Study of Anglo-American Sensibilities* (London: Hamish Hamilton, 1974), p. xiii. It is remarkable that no equivalent study has been undertaken in Anglo-Irish or Irish-American literary and cultural sensibilities.

[38] In Seamus Heaney's terms: "The landscape was sacramental, instinct with signs, implying a system of reality beyond the visible realities." 'The Sense of Place' (1974) in *Preoccupations: Selected Prose 1968-1978* (London: Faber and Faber, 1980), p. 132.
[39] *The Figure in the Cave*, p. 210. 'The Impact of International Modern Poetry on Irish Writing' was originally broadcast on RTE radio as part of a series of talks, *Irish Poets in English*, and subsequently was published under that title in a collection edited by Sean Lucy (Cork: The Mercier Press, 1973).
[40] ibid., p. 211.
[41] ibid., p. 213.
[42] ibid., p. 216.
[43] ibid., p. 216.
[44] ibid., p. 216.
[45] ibid., p. 218.
[46] ibid., p. 219.
[47] *cf.* Seamus Heaney, *The Government of the Tongue* (London: Faber and Faber, 1988) and Seamus Deane, *Celtic Revivals* (London: Faber and Faber, 1985).
[48] Philip Larkin, *Required Writing: Miscellaneous Pieces 1955-1982* (London: Faber and Faber, 1983), p. 79. It is interesting to compare Larkin's remark with Heaney's comment in 'Feeling into Words' (1974): "... it is dangerous for a writer to become too self-conscious about his own processes: to name them too definitively may have the effect of confining them to what is named." *Preoccupations*, p. 52.
[49] From Montague's poem, 'Waiting': "some/Generous natural image of the good" in *The Great Cloak*, p. 56.
[50] To pick up again on Spender's terms of reference in *Love-Hate Relations*, p. xiii.
[51] See Loftus, *Nationalism in Modern Anglo-Irish Poetry*; in particular chapters 1, 2, 3 and 6.

10

Breathing Spaces

Brendan Kennelly

> There is no audience in Ireland, though I have managed to build up out of my need a little audience for myself. The real problem is the scarcity of a right audience which draws out of a poet what is best in him. The Irish audience that I came into contact with tried to draw out of me everything that was loud, journalistic and untrue.
>
> —Patrick Kavanagh, *Self-Portrait*

Much of what Brendan Kennelly has written is influenced, directly or indirectly, by the problem so boldly stated by Patrick Kavanagh in his *Self-Portrait* (1964). In particular, Kennelly's early poems, most of which are collected in the volume *Breathing Spaces* (1992), chart his growing unease and concern with making what he calls "connection":

> The sense of connection, when it occurs, feels like a stroke of great good luck. But with whom or what does it become even momentarily possible to connect?

The need, to quote Kavanagh again, "to build up ... a little audience for myself" is taken over by Kennelly as both a personal and a cultural mission. Kennelly's poetry inhabits the artistic ground where these two impulses collide.

Undoubtedly, this provocative intersection accounts for the extraordinary commitment Kennelly has shown during the 80s to give readings from his work, primarily in Ireland, but also abroad. It may also account for his willingness to speak on various moral and sexual issues which emerged in Ireland throughout the same period.

This high-profile public persona was indeed consummated in

Kennelly's book-length poems, or epics, *Cromwell* and *The Book of Judas,* and has certainly contributed enormously to Kennelly's vast popular reputation in Ireland.

In the earlier work, such as *Love Cry* (1972), *Islandman* (1977), *A Small Light* (1979), *A Girl* (1981) and in the previously uncollected poems gathered in the title section, *Breathing Spaces,* one sees the extent to which Kennelly has been preoccupied with these polemical issues of audience and the poet's place in a society such as Ireland—so very traditional in ways, and yet brashly, almost aggressively, engaged by the new.

What makes *Breathing Spaces* particularly revealing is that, in the introduction and notes accompanying each section of the book, Kennelly alludes to a deep anxiety about the fault-lines which run between the traditional, community life in Ireland and its demise. It is an anxiety Kavanagh would have well understood.

In a sense, Kennelly is to the Republic of the 80s what Kavanagh was to the Republic of the 40s and 50s. Both poets are haunted by bardic nostalgia; both are suspicious of high-brow pretensions about 'Art'; both are mindful of the subversiveness of the comic spirit and both respect the rhetorical wisdom of anecdote and folklore. Indeed, while much has been made of Seamus Heaney's intellectual appropriation of Kavanagh's example, we should bear in mind the equally important cultural similarities which Brendan Kennelly shares with Kavanagh.

To take even the most obvious of examples: both poets come from a small-town/rural village background, the familiarity of which led to a sense of spiritual shock and personal difficulty when confronted by city life. This breakdown is recorded in the poems with pathos, bitterness, and, sometimes, self-mockery.

Kavanagh's distaste for Dublin's literary life is, of course, legendary. "I wasted what could have been my four glorious years," Kavanagh recalls in *Self-Portrait,* "begging and scrambling around the streets of malignant Dublin."

The experience of leaving behind the known, identifiable world of Inniskeen for Dublin in 1939, and the kind of personal distortions and loss that this change seems to have brought about in Kavanagh's psyche is a dominant theme in his poetry. It is also the focus for *Self-Portrait* and provides the radical poignancy to Kavanagh's life and work as a poet:

> Round about the late 1930s a certain prosperity came through and foolishly enough that was the time I chose to leave my native fields. I had no messianic impulse to leave. I was happy. I went against my will. A lot of our actions are like that. We miss the big emotional gesture and drift away. Is it possible to achieve our potential grand passion? I believe so. Perhaps that has been my weakness.

Kavanagh's Monaghan provided him with what he called "the right simplicity" which he had to rediscover ("back to where I started") in order to achieve "weightlessness"—the unforced, indifferent mystery which is the hallmark of true poetry.

The Kerry and Shannon where Kennelly grew up during the 40s and early 50s provide him with rich local detail, landscape, stories and the very simplicity of language which characterises *Breathing Spaces.*

Like Kavanagh, Kennelly records the transition of the individual from having a defined and definite place in a community, to another world of broken and fractured identities wherein 'the self' is effectively unknowable in the received and hierarchic terms of the parish. The self becomes, instead, the site of 'egotism', a deeply suspect force in Kennelly's lexicon.

Kennelly's uncertainty in addressing the self is matched by Kavanagh's reticence: "I dislike talking about myself in a direct way. The self is only interesting as an illustration" is how Kavanagh opens his *Self-Portrait.* Similarly, Kennelly states in his note to *Islandman*:

> Through an act of sustained and deliberate indirectness, it is possible to say more completely whatever one has to say. It is one of the fertile paradoxes of poetry that one can be more candid by engaging less in frontalism and by listening more keenly to the voices of the personae in the wings.

Throughout the introduction and in the notes to the individual volumes of *Breathing Spaces,* Kennelly is troubled by 'the self'. It is a "mobile, boggy swamp of egotism and dull confusion"—a phrase which he repeats—and he refers later to the "monstrous yet magnificient energies of egotism". Other references include the *mere* self, the *messy* self, all by way of disentangling the one moral and artistic problem which Kennelly clearly sees as being paramount to his own identity as a writer: "I sometimes think that poetry takes the mickey out of poets ... The problem is to keep the egolife from mauling the poemlife." Indeed, poetry threatens to become a *substitute* for the self, an alternative life almost, which bridges the past, and its known community (an inherited audience, in effect), with the present atomised reality.

Many of the poems in *Breathing Spaces* literally document, sociologically, anthropologically, the traditional community, as in *Love Cry*, a sequence of 40 sonnets. The poems name a place or person, tell stories and relate the passing of a way of life. It is poetry as lament. While conscious of the brute realities of farming, Kennelly dramatises the beauty of the landscape wherein his 'characters' live out their lives. Little is gone into, but the sufficient exterior of *Love Cry* reveals a terrifying cycle of acceptance, tinged with regret and, often, curtailed rage, as in 'Spring':

Curtin spent the winter in the County Home
And drank and whored and gambled in the spring;
I met him once, the black days coming on,
He told me straight that he was going in.
'Last night,' he said, 'I left a farmer's house,
The moon was up, a wicked light abroad,
The innocent roads were turning treacherous
And ice, you know, is the pure cruelty of God.

Well, soon enough, I'll meet the men who fail
At everything poor Christian men esteem.
Down-hearted villians! You should hear them sing!
Homeless as crows, yet they keep body and soul
Together. Just like me. Know what I mean?
The winter within walls. And then—the spring!'

The poem displays the characteristic attributes of *Breathing Spaces*: the encounter, the conversation, the voice, the closure: "And then—the spring!". What is so noticeable about *Breathing Spaces* is the extent to which the poems, ranging over 20 years, are shadowed by death, pain and loss.

It is as if, deprived of the defined communal world, the poet finds recompense in the language and social conditions of the past, only to realise that these no longer exist and that the world-view they embody has fragmented and is, effectively, dead. How else is one to account for the (almost) obsessive preoccupation of the poems with death, dying, ghosts, and the adequacy of poetry to convey such experience?

> The fields were strewn with dead metaphors.
> Language had fought a pitched battle and lost.

Physical death is omnipresent in *Breathing Spaces.* There is too the notion that failure, as another form of death, must be acknowledged by the poetic imagination since nothing should be repugnant to the poet. "Failure is your daily bread." "[It] is the source/Of all our celebration", as Kennelly remarks in 'Failure' and concludes the poem:

> I will look at all this, loving it
> As I have always loved it,
> Feeling the failure rise like the tide,
> Waves wasting their perfection
> On my ignorant shores.

So the poet becomes an icon of authentic life, taking everything 'in' and by that very fact celebrating life in the teeth of denial, repression and insufficiency. This late-Romantic notion, conditioned by the joking, devilish quality in the poetic personae, finds straightforward endorsement in Kennelly's introductory note to 'Islandman':

> I want to love every heartbeat, every musical second of happiness and grief, boredom and fun and the usual no-man's-land of viable and reasonably rewarded half-being, permitted between stoneself and definitive dust. Whatever forces help one to love this frequently muted music of time are to be welcomed by imagination and intelligence, body and soul. Whatever or whoever you are, be with me now.

The yearning here ("be with me now") does have a religious dimension to it because poetry becomes a form of secular Mass, compensating for the deadliness of institutional spirituality. Kennelly's poetry, after all, depicts the lives of the victims of the Irish Catholic Church. Such failure hangs like a cultural fate against which the characters of Kennelly's poems sometimes rail, mock, but often accept with inarticulate cries from the heart.

> Ritchie screamed to see his chastised son

So changed, as though the quick rebuke
Had driven him to a world unknown.
But now he lay there, still, beyond all pain;
The village watched and wept while Ritchie shook,
Two women pressed eager lips upon
Blue lips, giving their kiss of life. In vain.

In this sense, then, the poet is looked to as a figure who can strike back, if symbolically, at the forces of moral, sexual and political containment: "Ireland," Kennelly writes in his introduction, "is, above all, the Land of the Label, a green kingdom of clichés. To write poetry in Ireland is to declare war on labels and clichés." The poem is a coded message which confirms in the reader's (or audience's) mind that the poet knows what is going on, because he has suffered the same kind of repression as his audience. The poem is a vehicle of this identification. Such knowledge is not, however, absolute and incontrovertible. As Kennelly remarks in the headnote to *Love Cry*:

> I showed some of these poems to an old man from the place in which most of the poems are set. He read them and said vehemently, 'Lies! Lies! Poetry is all bloody lies!' He paused, then added, much more gently, 'But a poet's lies can make a man look twice at himself and the world.'

What Kennelly has achieved in the poems of *Breathing Spaces* is to keep an accessible channel of communication open between himself and the wider public in whose name his poems are written. He has *recreated* that audience in the image of what they once were and he has been able to maintain this relationship by exploiting the language of church-ritual and common speech with total ease.

I touch the stones.
My mother smiles, my father dances,
My daughter peppers me with questions,
A swimmer finds his music, an ambulance screams
In mercy, I build a bridge of love,
The willow speaks, the lightning dreams,
The blackbird sings, I make a wish, the gift appears
To bless this art
    that deepens friendship
        through the years.

The force of poetic personality, the telling accent of the spoken line, has meant that Kennelly's poems are essentially available as stories. In this he has kept faith with his forebears, a loyalty which marks almost every poem in *Breathing Spaces* and the ideological commitment which Kennelly declares in 'A Small Light':

> Today the idea of community is vanishing fast; what we witness for the most part, in the efforts of those who try to create them, are, however admirable the impulses behind the efforts, sad parodies of community.

Kennelly's poetry is painfully aware of the parody and the unavoidable reality that the idea of community, which he reimagines in his writing, is literally *vanishing*. What exactly the idea of that community is will provide historians and cultural critics with a tantalising glimpse of an Ireland which might have been; elusively present in the voices, feelings and attitudes of Kennelly's country-folk, "the personae in the wings".

For all the brashness and ebullience of *Breathing Spaces*, there is a Lorca-like recognition of darkness and death and an anger at the modern world:

> Is the contemporary poet, by definition, a part-timer, one who with a grateful sigh settles down to try to write when the fierce trivialities have for the moment been coped with? He is so often a voice without an audience, an endured oddity, an articulate freak with oddball values, a stone , a severed head, a voice in a void.

This is plain as a pikestaff and it lays down Kennelly's just claim to be considered alongside those other poets in these islands, such as Tony Harrison, who attempt to restore the poet to some kind of public life.

Certainly Kennelly's unflagging energy in producing poetry which is popular (in the sense of being directed at the people) underlines his critical relationship with Patrick Kavanagh. As Kavanagh remarked in one of the finest passages of *Self-Portrait*:

> I had been assailing the myth of Ireland by which they were managing to beat the artistic rap. I had seen and shewn that this Ireland thing was an undignified business—the trade of enemies and failures.

In the major poems which followed the collections gathered in

Breathing Spaces, Brendan Kennelly assails "the myth of Ireland" with a vengeance. The anticipations, echoes and soundings which one hears in *Love Cry*, *A Small Light* or 'Shelley in Dublin' are, in retrospect, unmistakable preparations for the war of words, the operatic thunder and 'fabulous fact' of Kennelly's greatest poetic achievements to date—*Cromwell* and *The Book of Judas*.

* The poetry quoted in this chapter is taken from Brendan Kennelly, *Breathing Spaces: Early Poems* (Bloodaxe Books, Newcastle-upon-Tyne, 1992).

11

Icon and Lares

Michael Longley and Derek Mahon

In the opening essay of his book, *The World, the Text, and the Critic*[1], Edward Said quotes approvingly Ian Watt's comment on Joseph Conrad's contemporaries: "writers like Lawrence, Joyce and Pound who present us with 'the breaking of ties with family, home, class and country, and traditional beliefs as necessary stages in the achievement of spiritual and intellectual freedom' ... invite us to share the larger transcendental ... or private systems of order and value which they have adopted and invented."[2] According to Said, these transcendental values are "affiliative", whereas the family, home, class and country ties are "filiative":

> What I am describing is the transition from a failed idea or possibility of filiation to a kind of compensatory order that, whether it is a party, an institution, a culture, a set of beliefs, or even a world-vision, provides men and women with a new form of relationship, which I have been calling affiliation but which is also a new system.[3]

The transition to which Said refers is, I think, central to a discussion of Irish literature and tradition and the history which has determined the development of both. Specifically in regard to Irish poetry, Said's comments offer a perspective on two of the country's most accomplished living poets, Michael Longley and Derek Mahon. I would like to relate their achievement as poets to this theme: that personal search for a compensatory order to transcend those "ties" of "family, home, class and country" with which their poetry often deals, and which in Ireland is more customarily called history.

At the outset, I think it is fair to distinguish between the two poets on one crucial issue; whereas Longley's poetry seeks to embrace history, to restore the ties of family, home, class and country, Mahon rebukes such a possibility, discovering in the imagination an alternative home that transcends what he perceives as the failed filiative bonds. This central distinction between their work finds a literary precedent in the figure of Louis MacNeice. For it was he who sought a balance between an acceptance and a rejection of his northern Protestant past, together with a deeper understanding of the modern world and what place the imagination could find in it. Both younger poets have, earlier in their writing lives, referred to Louis MacNeice: he is "a touchstone of what an Ulster poet might be"[4] according to Longley, while, for Mahon, MacNeice's exclusion "from the charmed circle ... of Irish Poets" is as a result of his failure to express the national aspirations which "after all, include patriotic graft and pious baloney". Mahon then elaborates:

> There are several attempts in the early poems [of MacNeice] to establish an Irish persona, but none is very convincing. Ryan, in 'Eclogue from Iceland', describes himself as an 'exile', but there is a measure of disingenuousness here. 'Exile', in the histrionic and approximate sense in which the word is used in Ireland, was an option available to Joyce and O'Casey, who 'belonged' to the people from whom they wished to escape. *It was not available, in the same sense, to MacNeice, whose background was a mixture of Anglo-Irish and Ulster Protestant (C of I).* Whatever his sympathies he didn't, by class or religious background, 'belong to the people'. How then, not sharing the general constraints, could he free himself from them?[5] [my italics]

It is a frank acknowledgement of MacNeice's distance from an official 'Irish tradition' and 'the people' of whom it was, in part, created. 'Exile' is then an inaccurate term, as Mahon says, since MacNeice did not 'belong' in the first place. The matter is taken up by Michael Longley in 'My Protestant Education':[6]

> The grammar school I moved onto had enjoyed a radical reputation in the 19th century, and it remained a tolerant and pleasantly secular place. There I encountered that tough scepticism and disenchanted liberalism with which many educated and moderate Protestants who cannot accept either Nationalism or diehard Unionism fill the vacuum—qualities which have been most deeply articulated in the imagination of Louis MacNeice.

With MacNeice being so central a figure in both Mahon's and Longley's sense of creative identity, it is hardly surprising that their own poems register many of the explicit themes with which MacNeice dealt, such as the life of the city, history, family, love, nature and the west of Ireland. These recurrent motifs convey, I think, the tension, uncertainty and shifting focus of both poets' reaction to 'belonging'[7], to creating a tradition in which they can feel at home. It is instructive, therefore, to note briefly some of the dominant literary figures, other than MacNeice, who appear in their work as illustration of the traditions with which they identify.

With Longley, it is an acknowledged 'English' literary tradition that includes Edward Thomas, Samuel Johnson, John Clare, the World War I poets; with Mahon, beyond the interest of the early poems in De Quincey and 'decadents' like Dowson, it is the austerities of Beckett and Cavafy, Pasternak and Brecht, the displaced Modernists, Pound, Lewis and Madox Ford[8], that attract the poet the most. Similarly, to look at the visual artists who have inspired the poets: one sees L.S. Lowry and Gerard Dillon in Longley, while Van Gogh and Uccello prefigure in Mahon's work. These differences between the poets, illustrative of their naturally separate identities as poets, also suggest their different responses, attitudes and beliefs, shaped by what Derek Mahon has described as their being

> ... Protestant products of an English educational system, with little or no knowledge of the Irish language and an inherited duality of cultural reference. They are a group apart, but need not be considered in isolation, for their very difference assimilates them to the complexity of the continuing Irish past.[9]

It is around this 'duality', and the contrasting ways in which the two poets imaginatively cope with it that the fact of their northern Protestantism is pivotal. It is a distinctiveness that implies distance from those other standard cultural references, English and Irish. Yet it also involves a separation from 'their own' northern Protestantism which bears the taint of bigotry and hate. These are important factors in an understanding of the imaginative orientation of Michael Longley and Derek Mahon.

With Longley, there is a recording both of this cultural distinctiveness and of *its* relationship with, and exposure to, Irish social and physical settings. Mahon, however, includes this distinctiveness as a statement of the modern poetic sensibility, cut adrift but still implicated in some way with the historical world from which it emerged. Consequently, one finds in many of Mahon's poems the poet, looking on, spectatorial, whereas Longley is out and about in the world of his poems, amazed by nature's delicacy, the landscape of the past, making connections that Mahon remains unconvinced of, and often removed from. Out of a common impulse towards solitude, accepted as an almost inevitable condition of their own artistic individuality, the poets reach markedly different conclusions. To take an example, the contrast between Mahon's 'The Attic'[10] and Longley's 'Weather'[11], presents each poet's characteristic stance. With Mahon, a cityscape gives way to "At work in your attic/Up here under the roof" and the poet's sequestered imagination: "Silent by ticking lamplight/I stare at the blank spaces."

In such exemplary isolation, the poet-figure seems in a self-accusatory mood, closing down the circuits to the world outside:

> I who know nothing
> Scribbling on the off-chance,
> Darkening the white page,
> Cultivating my ignorance.

Mahon's "Muse-light on the city" is a kind of watchtower, beleaguered by enemies from both within and without. In 'Weather', Longley's demeanour is, in contrast, typically active, in this instance carrying buckets of water indoors:

> ... heavy
>
> Under the pressure of
> Enormous atmospheres,
> Two lakes and the islands
> Enlarging constantly ...

If the "world of heightened sense" is in Mahon's 'The Attic' precisely that—an abstracted thing—Longley's amazement, interest, love and need to detail such a world literally knows no bounds:

> ... I shelter
> Landmarks, keep track of

Animals, all the birds
In a reduced outdoors ...

The final stanza of 'Weather' begins with a telling gesture:

And open my windows,
The wings of dragonflies
Hung from an alder cone,
A raindrop enclosing
Brookweed's five petals.

The "five petals", suggesting the complete range of human senses, are caught up exclusively in the naturalistic fact and the wonderful exchange whereby the poet reveals its beauty. Longley ends up facing the world, whereas Mahon is facing the page. So while Longley takes the natural world to heart and humanises it in the process, Mahon's denatured world is calmly mindful, brooding on itself.

In each case, and several other poems such as Mahon's 'Jail Journal' or Longley's 'Alibis', could further illustrate the point, the poets' self-consciousness leads in opposite directions. Yet the objective is similar: to discover some kind of truth that can stand up for itself *as poetry*. Like MacNeice, both poets seek to create a community of realisable values that are personally authentic and yet generally available, such as those seen to be present in nature: particularly in the redemptive landscapes of the west of Ireland. We can relate these clusters of ideas and images throughout the poetry of Michael Longley and Derek Mahon to clarify where their differences as poets lie, and how they yet derive from the background they have in common (Protestant Belfast)[12], but also to recognise how these differences are assimilated to "the continuing Irish past".

Take, for instance, the concluding stanza of Mahon's 'The Spring Vacation', dedicated to Longley:

One part of my mind must learn to know its place.
The things that happen in the kitchen houses
And echoing back-streets of this desperate city
Should engage more than my casual interest,
Exact more interest than my casual pity[13]

and the final lines of his 'Afterlives':

But the hills are still the same
Grey-blue above Belfast.
Perhaps if I'd stayed behind
And lived it bomb by bomb
I might have grown up at last
And learnt what is meant by home.[14]

The sense of incompleteness in the second poem recalls the earlier ambiguity, and resistance to the filiative emotion that "this desperate city" (of Belfast) cannot "engage". Against this, one can place Longley's 'In Memory of Gerard Dillon' which lovingly portrays one of the city's finest painters:

You are a room full of self-portraits,
A face that follows us everywhere;
An ear to the ground listening for
Dead brothers in layers; an eye
Taking in the beautiful predators—
Cats on the windowsill, birds of prey
And, between the diminutive fields,
A dragonfly, wings full of light
Where the road narrows to the last farm.[15]

Whereas Mahon is working out his relation to the city as an artist, Longley subsumes this problem in the concrete details with which his poem ends:

Christening robes, communion dresses,
The shawls of factory workers,
A blind drawn on the Lower Falls.[16]

This difference, which can be roughly viewed as that between the abstract question and the concrete detail, between "what is meant by home" and "A blind drawn on the Lower Falls", is present in the contrasting ways the two poets define their own immediate family backgrounds. Longley's 'In Memoriam', for instance, records his father's death, a long-delayed consequence of World War I:

Finally, that lousy war was over.
Stranded in France and in need of proof
You hunted down experimental lovers,

Persuading chorus girls and countesses:
This, father, the last confidence you spoke.
In my twentieth year your old wounds woke
As cancer.[17]

And in the better-known 'Wounds', the "pictures from my father's head" coalesce with images of the current Northern Irish conflict:

I bury beside him
Three teenage soldiers, bellies full of
Bullets and Irish beer, their flies undone.
A packet of Woodbines I throw in,
A lucifer, the Sacred Heart of Jesus
Paralysed as heavy guns put out
The night-light in a nursery for ever ...[18]

Compared with these family biographies[19], full of personal history, Derek Mahon's 'Grandfather', 'My Wicked Uncle', 'A Refusal to Mourn' and 'Father-in-Law' read as meditations on a theme removed from the complexly human:

I think we would have had a lot in common—
Alcohol and the love of one woman
Certainly; but I failed the eyesight test
When I tried for the Merchant Navy,
And lapsed into this lyric lunacy.
When you lost your balance like Li Po
They found unfinished poems in your sea-chest.[20]

The focus shifts away from the man, the father-in-law, to the significance of those "unfinished poems" and how they tie in with Mahon's self-consciousness over his own "lyric lunacy". Similarly, the figure in 'A Refusal to Mourn',[21] who "Once a week ... would visit/An old shipyard crony" becomes, like 'My Wicked Uncle'[22], a carrier of a more abstract significance, in his case concerning time and man's place in the proceedings. These characters challenge the community out of which they come in a way similar to the poet's own art and irony. They are renegades, like the poet, raiding the inarticulate and respectable Protestant anonymity or, like the worker in 'A Refusal to Mourn', they become testaments to the positive side of that community and its persistence:

In time the astringent rain
Of those parts will clean
The words from his gravestone
In the crowded cemetery
That overlooks the sea
And his name be mud once again

And his boilers lie like tombs
In the mud of the sea bed
Till the next ice age comes
And the earth he inherited
Is gone like Neanderthal Man
And no records remain.

But the secret bred in the bone
On the dawn strand survives
In other times and lives,
Persisting for the unborn
Like a claw-print in concrete
After the bird has flown.

This lyrical rhetoric, bearing witness to the man's meaning as "the secret bred in the bone/... Persisting for the unborn", is one of the crucial points at which Mahon and Longley part company from the backgrounds they have in common, to view that background and the worlds from which it is separated through different ends of the telescope. This divergence can be seen at various levels, which should be considered before the question of how, in spite of these differences, both poets relate to "the continuing Irish past".

In 'Autobiographies'[23], Derek Mahon depicts his sense of himself as a child "While the frozen armies trembled/At the gates of Leningrad". The poem, in four sections, portrays through images of still reclamation the social radii of Mahon's growing-up. "But who can re-live their lives?" he enquires in 'The Lost Girls' and, in the third and fourth sections of 'Autobiographies'[24], the poem revolves around a questioning uncertainty of identity that is characteristic of Mahon's poetry as a whole:

Years later; the same dim
Resort has grown dimmer
As if some centrifugal
Force, summer by summer,

Has moved it ever farther
From an imagined centre.

(3: The Last Resort)

... its wheels still sing
In the memory, stars that turn
About an eternal centre,
The bright spokes glittering.

(4: The Bicycle)

The imagined, eternal centre[25] of repose and equilibrium of balance is the poet's own sense of an artistic consciousness, the position of being "(I must have been four then)/... held up to the window/For a victory parade—". That status of observer, removed from 'reality' but yet part of it, predominates in Mahon's poetry, making of the poems a sustained enquiry into the relationship between the poet and the historical world.[26] The moments of experience and recollection, like the landscapes in which these take place, are secondary to Mahon's primary concern: to understand the imagination and find a place for *it* in the modern world. This artistic self-consciousness is directly related to Mahon's cultural inheritance which he views as being antagonistic to art by its very nature.

This contrasts sharply with Michael Longley. For while Longley also questions the role and relevance of poetry, his very indirection masks, through the sheer force of 'ordinary' detail and its concentration as 'artfulness', the uncertainty and ambivalence that influence his self-awareness as a poet. It is, one feels, a question of acceptance and rejection similar to that which MacNeice experienced. Longley has accepted his past (the Protestant city, the cultural 'duality', the shaky identity), whereas Mahon has rejected his. MacNeice's spiritual sons have gone their different ways: one has remained at home, the other has left.

In this regard, Mahon's attitude to Belfast as the 'Protestant' city and the way in which 'British', or more correctly English, elements influence Longley, cast some light on both poets' sense of artistic identity. It is significant that Longley's chosen literary antecedents—Dr Johnson, John Clare, Edward Thomas, Isaac Rosenberg—relate problematically to the English tradition. They are, that is to say, outsiders in English terms, excluded on various grounds like the 'mad' peasant Clare, the Jewish Rosenberg. Even Johnson's relationship to the dominant aristocratic tradition of his time was as a combatively independent spokesman for the 'ordinary' cultured man. It is a loosely assembled gallery, an aesthetic and moral order to which Longley affiliates *inside* the English literary tradition. Its virtues, ambitions, experience and beliefs are of such a kind that Longley can give imaginative assent to them without simultaneously undermining his commitment, emotional as much as artistic, to the Northern Irish experience that shaped him. One makes sense of the other, as in the homage to his "Jewish granny":

> I tilt her head towards you, Isaac Rosenberg,
> But can you pick out that echo of splintering glass
> From under the bombardment, and in No Man's Land
> What is there to talk about but difficult poems?[27]

The familial dimension, which profoundly underlies Longley's literary sense of England, breeds recurrent, haunting images of elusive ancestors:

> Late travellers on the Underground
> People my head like a ghost town.[28]

In a sense, Longley's background echoes the historical experience of the Ulster Protestant as immigrant, since his parents moved from London to Belfast in the late 20s, more than a decade before his birth. In 'Dr Johnson on the Hebrides', with London "so far", the poet finds a stabilising focus in the great Augustan who

> trudges off in the mist and the rain
> Where only the thickest skin survives,
> Among the rocks construes himself again,
> Lifts through those altering perspectives
>
> His downcast eyes, riding out the brainstorm,
> His weatherproof enormous head at home.[29]

Mahon's poems rarely resolve in being "at home", because Belfast and Protestant Ulster are rejected. The poet, contaminated by Protestant Ulster's deadly pieties, finds that, in spite of it all, the gestures, accents and postures can still exert their hold over him:

God, you could do it, God
help you, stand on a corner stiff
with rhetoric, promising nothing under the sun.[30]

'You could but can't' seems to echo behind the lines of the poem. This is not to say that Mahon banishes that past and place out of his poems. Far from it. He has instead sought different ways of incorporating it; for instance, in 'Courtyards in Delft'[31] 17th-century Dutch art transposes the poet's own background and makes it accessible to his imagination:

... this is life too, and the cracked
Out-house door a verifiable fact
As vividly mnemonic as the sunlit
Railings that front the houses opposite.

I lived there as a boy and know the coal
Glittering in its shed, late-afternoon
Lambency informing the deal table,
The ceiling cradled in a radiant spoon.
I must be lying low in a room there,
A strange child with a taste for verse,
While my hard-nosed companions dream of fire
And sword upon parched veldt and fields of rain-swept gorse.

Furthermore, in poems like 'Nostalgias' and 'Songs of Praise', Mahon unpicks "the parochial lives we might have led,/Praising a stony god who died before our time"[32]; while his sense of the wider historical context of Ulster Scots Protestant experience embraces, in 'Canadian Pacific'[33], their neglected exodus "From famine, pestilence and persecution":

Those gaunt forefathers shipped abroad to find
Rough stone of heaven beyond the western ocean,
And staked their claim, and pinned their faith.

Two separate but complementary perspectives emerge, then, from which Longley's and Mahon's common inheritance (of Protestant Ulster) is viewed: one looking towards possible 'English' parallels, while the other looks inwards, at the very nature of that inheritance. Mahon introduces in his poem 'Teaching in Belfast'[34] another crucial element in this exploration. As "the lunch hour nears its end",

This is the moment my fantasy begins
And I drive with a generous lady, long since lost,
Against the traffic to the glittering west,
Startling the hens in drowsy villages,
Cushioned with money, time and privileges.

It is useful to see just how "the glittering west" of Ireland features in their work. For both poets, but particularly for Longley, the west of Ireland is seen as an embodiment of some kind of alternative life, a fictional life that compensates for certain values and attitudes missing in the real, given, historical world. For Longley, the west is a "home from home"[35]; for Mahon, 'Thinking of Inis Oírr in Cambridge, Mass.'[36], it is the "Reflection in that final sky" which "Shames vision into simple sight":

I clutch the memory still, and I
Have measured everything with it since.

Longley itemises that vision into the simple sights of landscape and nature which, common to the west of Ireland, take on in his work a symbolic potency all of their own. To accommodate this and, one senses, to earth it, Longley describes what he sees as the human story (as in 'Mayo Monologues')[37] but he also recreates a world of and for his imagination. The effort does not go without its own sense of characteristic self-mocking:

... by the time I am accepted there
(A reputation and my own half-acre)
I shall have written another letter home.[38]

There or *here*? The implicit conflict is between home (*here*)—the family place, the place of all those unasked-for ties and commitments (*lares* as Longley calls them), the implicated ideas and beliefs one has no part in making but simply by being 'from here' is responsible for—and the recreated place, the place of the imagination, symbol and icon—*there*. The conflict between these two conditions runs consistently throughout Longley's poetry and, in his 'Letter to Derek Mahon'[39], his almost mystical appropriation of Inis Oírr just about gives way to the commonsensical concluding lines:

> ... yes,
> We would have lingered there for less ...
> Six islanders for a ten-bob note
> Rowed us out to the anchored boat.

The west of Ireland, in other words, whether it be Mayo or the Aran Islands, exists *between* reality and the imagination, a "dream world"[40] as MacNeice called it, a testing ground, a possibility and a means by which other experiences, other histories can be gauged.

Where Longley and Mahon differ is, again, on the inverse terms of their reference. This is Mahon's 'Aran':

> Scorched with a fearful admiration
> Walking over the nacreous sand,
> I dream myself to that tradition,
> Fifty winters off the land—[41]

The dream remains a *dream*, whereas Longley seeks to realise and understand this world[42], to "put their district on the map/And to name the fields for them".[43] Longley's ambition, full of risks of being misinterpreted, involves an imaginative dialogue and an acknowledgement of what is distinctive, not alone in the poet himself, but in the Other, be that found in physical, social or cultural terms. Between the poles of this exchange, the current of his poetic imagination is charged and it, in turn, becomes a means of revitalisation. With Mahon, the actual means of discourse, from his own 'self' to his past and the imaginative world he has created, is stripped and its working order laid bare. Longley's aesthetic act becomes moral, as does Mahon's, precisely at the point where it has been considered to ascend into a rarefied form of indifference.

This is Stan Smith's reading, in *Inviolable Voice*[44]:

> ... a poetry that looks back to the sceptical Protestant tradition of Louis MacNeice takes up a worried, disapproving but finally uncomprehending stance towards an experience with which it feels no sense of affinity.

This poetry, Smith suggests,

> ... performs its civil duties equitably, by reflecting in an abstracted kind of way, on violence, but [keeps] its hands ... indubitably clean. It speaks, at times, with the tone of a shell-shocked Georgianism that could easily be mistaken for indifference before the ugly realities of life, and death, in Ulster.

It is probably unwise for a critic to arm himself with such claims when judging writers who actually confront, by living through, "the ugly realities of life, and death, in Ulster" as Michael Longley has done since the beginning of the present Troubles. It is also unclear, in the first quotation, what *experience* Stan Smith is referring to before which "the sceptical Protestant tradition ... takes up a worried, disapproving but finally uncomprehending stance". Experience of the last two decades in Northern Ireland, of brutality, sectarianism and political failure, leaves little room for the imagination to heal that deep division between poet and history which Smith so effectively charts elsewhere in his important book. It is fairer to say that Derek Mahon and Michael Longley provide rich and ample illustration of the way in which poetry can, without losing any of its integral power and meaning, reaffirm basic human values (of hope, care, love and tolerance) when these self-same values are threatened, generally through the force of emasculated political will.

Derek Mahon relays his response with an understated discernment when he writes:

> The war I mean is not, of course, between Protestant and Catholic but between the fluidity of a possible life ... and the *rigor mortis* of archaic postures, political and cultural. The poets themselves have taken no part in political events, but they have contributed to that possible life, or the possibility of that possible life; for the act of writing is itself political in the fullest sense. A good poem is a paradigm of good politics—of people talking to each other, with honest subtlety, at a profound level. It is a light to lighten the darkness; and we have darkness enough, God knows, for a long time.[45]

The possiblity to which Mahon refers is that "new form of relationship ... and new system" described by Said. Mahon seeks to find or create it away from those ties of family, home, class and country, following such modern masters as Samuel Beckett. With Longley, one senses a reordering of those ties; an attempt to reform and preserve them as it were from the inside. Yet the root from which both ambitions grow and are eventually determined is the possibility of a place to call *home*, between what one needs and what one knows. It is a condition Michael Longley foresaw in one of his early poems, 'To Derek Mahon', re-entitled 'Birthmarks':

> Though we deny them name and birth,
> Locked out from rhyme and lexicon
> The ghosts still gather round our hearth
> Whose bed and board makes up the whole—
> Thief, murderer and clown—icon
> And lares of the poet's soul.[46]

Notes

[1] Edward W. Said, 'Introduction: Secular Criticism', in *The World, the Text, and the Critic* (London: Faber and Faber, 1984).
[2] ibid., p. 19. The Ian Watt quotation comes from his *Conrad in the Nineteenth Century* (Berkeley: University of California Press, 1979), p. 32.
[3] Said, p. 19.
[4] Michael Longley, *Causeway: The Arts in Ulster* (The Arts Council of Northern Ireland with Gill and Macmillan, 1971), p. 97. See also 'A Misrepresented Poet', in *Dublin Magazine*, Vol. 6, No. 1 (Spring 1967).
[5] Derek Mahon, 'MacNeice in England and Ireland', in Terence Brown and Alec Reid (eds.) *Time Was Away: The World of Louis MacNeice*, (Dublin: Dolmen Press, 1974), p. 117.
[6] Longley, 'My Protestant Education', *New Statesman*, 10 August 1974, p. 219.
[7] Said, p. 8.
[8] Derek Mahon, *A Kensington Notebook* (London: Anvil Poetry Press, 1979), p. 102.
[9] Derek Mahon, *The Sphere Book of Modern Irish Poetry* (London: Sphere Books, 1972), p. 14.
[10] Derek Mahon, *Poems 1962-1978* (Oxford: Oxford University Press, 1979), p. 102.
[11] Michael Longley, *Poems 1963-1983* (Edinburgh: Salamander Press; Dublin: Gallery Books, 1985), p. 120.
[12] "There are many ways in which poets can be contrasted and compared, but in the Northern Irish situation ... there is an obvious line to be drawn ... the difference of religious background, as always in Ireland, is not so much important in itself as it is an indication of political, therefore national, therefore cultural allegiance, or lack of it." Derek Mahon, 'Poetry in Northern Ireland', *20th Century Studies*, No. 4 (November 1970), p. 92.
[13] Mahon, *Poems 1962-1978*, p. 4.
[14] ibid., p. 58.
[15] Longley, *Poems 1963-1983*, p. 95.
[16] ibid., p. 95.

[17] ibid., p. 49.
[18] ibid., p. 86.
[19] See also 'Second Sight' (p. 151) and 'The Third Light' (p. 200).
[20] Mahon, *Poems 1962-1978.*
[21] ibid., pp. 75-6.
[22] ibid., pp. 5-6.
[23] ibid., pp. 87-91.
[24] ibid., pp. 90-1.
[25] In the second section, 'The Lost Girls', the idea of a centre is conveyed by: "The lost girls in a ring/On a shadowy school playground/Like the nymphs dancing together/ In the *Allegory of Spring*" (ibid., p. 89).
[26] See 'The Attic' and stanzas 12-18 of 'The Sea in Winter', ibid., pp. 112-13.
[27] Longley, *Poems 1963-1983,* p. 199.
[28] ibid., p. 77.
[29] ibid., p. 55.
[30] Mahon, *Poems 1962-1978,* p. 31.
[31] Mahon, *The Hunt by Night* (Oxford University Press, 1982), pp. 9-10.
[32] Mahon, *Courtyards in Delft* (Dublin: Gallery Books, 1981), p. 17.
[33] Mahon, *Poems 1962-1978,* p. 25.
[34] ibid., pp. 31-2.
[35] Longley, *Poems 1963-1983,* p. 94.
[36] Mahon, *Poems 1962-1978,* p. 27.
[37] Longley, *Poems 1963-1983,* pp. 161-4.
[38] ibid., p. 99.
[39] ibid., p. 82-3.
[40] Louis MacNeice, *The Strings Are False* (London: Faber and Faber, 1965), p. 216.
[41] Mahon, *Poems 1963-1978,* p. 34.
[42] As in 'Mayo Monologues'.
[43] Longley, *Poems 1963-1983,* p. 140.
[44] Stan Smith, *Inviolable Voice: History and Twentieth-Century Poetry* (Dublin: Gill and Macmillan, 1982), p. 189.
[45] Mahon, 'Poetry in Northern Ireland' (see note 12 above), p. 93.
[46] Longley, *Poems 1963-1983,* p. 58.

12

The Suburban Night

Eavan Boland, Paul Durcan and Thomas McCarthy

Doubt still sharks
the close suburban night.

And all the lights I love
Leave me in the dark.

—Eavan Boland, 'Lights'

I

There is an unexplored world in the ways in which Irish writers, from James Joyce onwards, have indicted their country for failing to live up to the moral and cultural aspirations embodied in its history. This indictment, rooted in both the psychological make-up and the artistic ambition of the writer, is not simply an expression of the writer's dissatisfaction at failing to find a significant place for his-or-herself in Irish life, although such feelings may have influenced different writers from time to time. Rather, it takes the form of a basic imaginative search for self-definition. The writer *creates* his or her subject by probing the present, constructed as it is in Ireland out of the coalescing forces of social conservatism, cultural nationalism, political violence and religious hegemony. In this vortex, the artistic identity is made, not inherited.

In his own work, James Joyce sought to find out where and how a genuine, creative, independence of spirit could thrive in spite of the intransigent, comic, pathetic and unchanging obstacles which always seemed to stand in the way. In the dark, complicated and often trivial ordinariness of life in Ireland, Joyce's imagination saw how an individual was at the mercy of those very moral, religious and cultural authorities who said one thing while practising another, or assumed the absolute right to know what was best for the faithful. His writing is full of the victims of such duplicity, although he also sings the praises of those who, in their thoughts and actions, are defiant.

The Mr. Duffys, Bob Dorans, Farringtons, Chandlers and Gabriel Conroys of this world are spiritual victims, paralysed in one way or another by their failure to challenge the contradictory society in which they live. Bloom in *Ulysses* both embodies the contradictions and usurps them with his instinct to survive, duped as he may well be, but redeemed nevertheless by Molly's passionate love. Meanwhile, in both *A Portrait of the Artist* and *Ulysses*, Stephen Dedalus makes no bones about his disdain for those around him who have fallen for the easy answers of a life tailored to convention:

> Stephen watched the three glasses being raised from the counter as his father and his two cronies drank to the memory of their past. An abyss of fortune or temperament sundered him from them. His mind seemed older than theirs; it shone coldly on their strifes and happiness and regrets like a moon upon a younger earth.[1]

Through Stephen, Joyce manufactured the conditions of a life balanced on a knife-edge between the ordinary and the transcendent; the contaminations of the past are constantly evoked as a measure of the impoverished reality of the here and now. Stephen thus furnishes the exemplary model of the Irish artist. Yet it is worth noting that, throughout his life and writing, Joyce *also* registered, as Hélène Cixous has remarked, "a certain scorn for 'the poet' as merely passive dreamer": "Joyce maintained always an ambiguous attitude to poetry; it seems perfect for secret loves and for song, but is has nothing to do with that reality which is Joyce's main preoccupation."[2]

Eavan Boland, Paul Durcan and Thomas McCarthy have attempted to face poetry towards "that reality" which Joyce mapped out—of human domestic relations, love and sexuality—without losing sight of how these realities are determined by forces often greater than themselves. Boland, for instance, carries this tension into the 'self' of her poems; Durcan rebels against everything that reeks of possible compromising acquiescence, while McCarthy memorialises, in emblematic moments of family and personal history, the fact that the world is as it is, for good or ill, whether we like it or not.

II

To begin with, I would like to refer to an essay which Eavan Bol, published in *Studies* called 'The Woman Poet in a National Tradition'.[3] In this thoughtful and important essay, she discusses not "the most universal aspect of poetry: its aesthetics", but what she calls "the ethics of poetry":

> In countries where the tensions between a poet and his birthplace are inherited and established such ethics may remain an abstraction. But in other places, in Eastern Europe, in the emergent African states, in parts of Black Africa, where such relations remain in transition, poets come early to an awareness of ethics. They would at least recognise the issues raised by arguments in this essay. For Ireland, for women, they would substitute other names. But the underlying truth is unchangeable.

So what are these issues which Eavan Boland raises? I cannot go into great depth here about the different aspects of her argument relative to women poets, but the main thrust of what she says is directly relevant:

> The concept of nation, the existence and force of its inherited customs, its store of emblems and refrains lies in wait for any poet, ready to ambush and overcome complexity with simplification ... how do such simplications occur? They happen, I believe, because national traditions—the Irish one is just a single example of it—have the power to edit out human complexities which do not suit its own programme.

The "programme" is that political and cultural continuity which Irish nationalist idealism embodies and which, elsewhere in her essay, Eavan Boland exposes as the "fusion of the national and the feminine, the interpretation of one by the other". This results in the use of women as "ornamental icons and figments of national expression". Irish poets, writes Boland, "were not just dealing with emblems. They were also evading the real women of an actual past. Women whose silence their poetry should have broken". The poet's objective should be to break through that silence, to interrupt the programme. "A society, a nation, a literary tradition is always in danger of making up its communicable heritage from its visible elements. Women, as it happens, are not especially visible in Ireland."

For it was his own need to strike out through the "ornamental icons and figments of expression" that drove Joyce towards the creation of all those invisible, anonymous men in *Dubliners* and Leopold Bloom in *Ulysses.* The womanly physicality of Molly, set beside the shadowed, haunted directness and wisdom of Gretta Conroy in 'The Dead', show Joyce drawing upon his own experience and relationships and refusing "to edit out human complexities".

Curiously, too, Eavan Boland's comment that, as a woman poet, she feels herself isolated in many ways by and from the 'national traditions' brings to mind the young Stephen's perception when he "watched the three glasses being raised from the counter as his father and his two cronies drank to the memory of their past. An abyss of fortune or temperament sundered him from them". Their masculine introversion and fantasy are marvellously described by Hélène Cixous in the following terms:

> ... the other world is there, accessible to the initiated; to reach beyond apparent objectivity, one has to decipher the signs, to use one's eyes in order to surprise the double face of things and the double meaning of the signs. Thus all developments entail equivocation: the innocent exterior is the mask of a delicious perversity.[4]

Cathleen Ní Houlihan as harlot. But how are we to read the trickery of these signs, given the domineering, male equivalence known as the Irish 'literary tradition'? Boland writes,

> Marginality within a tradition, however painful, confers certain advantages. It allows the writer clear eyes and a quick critical sense. That critical perspective, in turn, may allow him to re-locate himself within that tradition which alienated him in the first place. I wanted to re-locate myself within the Irish poetic tradition.

As we can now see, Eavan Boland's poetry draws upon all three elements mentioned here: a sense of isolation (or "marginality"), "clear eyes" and "a quick critical sense".

III

Since the publication of her first volume, *New Territory*[5], in 1967, Eavan Boland's poems have become increasingly more conscious of themselves as counters in her attempt to 're-locate' herself within the Irish poetic tradition. In that early volume, Boland's intelligence showed itself in a clever, ingenious exchange with standard 'Irish' themes (such as exile in 'The Flight of the Earls') and literary traditions (as in the long retelling of 'The Winning of Etain'). The collection also includes poems about Irish poets, such as O'Rahilly and Yeats ('Yeats in Civil War'), while 'Belfast *vs.* Dublin', with its literary conceits, is dedicated to Derek Mahon. 'From the Painting *Back from Market* by Chardin' is the first of Boland's poems about paintings; in it she focuses upon the "peasant woman" and her treatment at the hands of the 18th-century French painter, famous for his domestic scenes and portraits, animated by great flashes of light. Boland describes the scene and comments:

> I think of what great art removes:
> Hazard and death, the future and the past,
> This woman's secret history and her loves—

A central preoccupation in Boland's work is the "woman's secret history", as 'Self-Portrait on a Summer Evening' (in *The Journey and Other Poems*) shows. The later poem collapses the distinction between "what great art removes" and life:

> Can't you feel it?
> Aren't you chilled by it?
> The way the late afternoon
> is reduced to detail—
>
> the sky that odd shape of apron—
>
> opaque, scumbled—
> the lazulis of the horizon becoming
> optical greys
> before your eyes
> before your eyes ...

The poet becomes "a woman/in the last summer light" of the painting (also by Chardin), and she enters the realm of art *as herself*:

> in my ankle-length
> summer skirt

crossing between
the garden and the house,
under the whitebeam trees,
keeping an eye on
the length of the grass,
the height of the hedge,
the distance of the children

I am Chardin's woman ...

This discovery and how it is achieved, "edged in reflected light,/ hardened by/the need to be ordinary", indicate the unpredictable progress of Eavan Boland's work as a poet.

Her second collection, *The War Horse*[6], kept faith with the kind of strained literariness of *New Territory* in only a few poems, such as the Audenesque 'Cyclist with Cut Branches' and the formal exercises of 'From the Irish of Pangur Ban' and 'Elegy for a Youth Changed to a Swan'. There is a rhetorical engagement with "this woman's secret history", but it remains at an abstract level of posing the issues ('The Law of Love') or of assembling an album of images ('Sisters' or 'The Family Tree'). While successful in their own terms, these poems lack imaginative conviction.

In *The War Horse*, this conviction is provided by the very fine poems which open the collection ('The Other Woman', 'The War Horse', 'Child of Our Time', 'A Soldier's Son' and 'The Famine Road') and those which close it ('Suburban Woman' and 'Ode to Suburbia'). The woman who moves through the scenes of these poems is lover, mother and wife, trapped by the conventional images of her role, and struggling to authenticate her own 'self' without simultaneously denying the credibility of either:

No magic here. Yet you encroach until
The shy countryside, fooled
By your plainness falls, then rises
From your bed changed, schooled
Forever by your skill,
Your compromises.

What exactly the cost is of such "compromises", Eavan Boland explores in the much-changed writing-style of *In Her Own Image*.[7] Suburbia shrinks to the individual woman's own 'self', and, as this focus intensifies, so too does the look of the poetry. In contrast to the strong, well-made poems of *New Territory* and *The War Horse*, with their purposeful lines, regular metres and rhymes, the poems of *In Her Own Image* are stripped down to urgent notes after the initial fully fledged proclamation of 'Tirade for the Mimic Muse':

You did protect yourself from horrors,
From the lizarding of eyelids
From the whiskering of nipples,
From the slow betrayals of our bedroom mirrors—
How you fled

The kitchen screw and the rack of labour,
The wash thumbed and the dish cracked,
The scream of beaten women,
The crime of babies battered,
The hubbub and the shriek of daily grief
That seeks asylum behind suburb walls ...

In Her Own Image represents a coming-out, an expression of the need to be heard and not just seen. It bears all the scars of a painful confrontation:

Make your face naked,
Strip your mind naked,
Drench your skin in a woman's tears.
I will wake you from your sluttish sleep.
I will show you true reflections, terrors.
You are the Muse of all our mirrors.
Look in them and weep.

The language is freed of all the traditional freight of literary consolation, and out of the sense of outrage the poems break through to a new, uncompromising idiom. They deal with drudgery, violence and self-hatred, anorexia, mastectomy, menstruation, and the woman's need to understand not only all these, but her own desire as well. This emerges in poems such as 'Solitary', which is about masturbation, and 'Exhibitionist', in which the woman shows herself who and what she is, in both a literal and figurative act of self-exposure:

This is my way,
to strip and strip
until

my dusk flush,
nude shade
hush

of hip,
back bone,
thigh

blacks light
and I
become the night.

In Her Own Image exculpates that "woman's secret history" and erupts into the apocalyptic image of 'Witching':

I will
reverse
their arson,

make
a pyre
of my haunch

and so
the last thing
they know

will be
the stench
of my crotch.

I'll singe

a page
of history
for these my sisters.

What Boland does so impressively here is to reveal "this thrash/and gimmickry/of sex/my aesthetic" ('Exhibitionist'), by undermining the conventional images of women that both sexes hide behind. "Myths", as Boland asserts in 'Making Up', "are made by men", from Cathleen Ní Houlihan *to* the whore.

This is only part of the secret story, however: the 'loves' of the woman in Chardin's painting constitute the other half of it. The Elizabethan-like 'Song', for example, reveals the mystic of sexuality in another disguise:

Round as a bracelet
Clasping the wet grass,
An adder drowsed by berries
Which change blood to cess;
Dreading delay's venom
I risked the first kiss.

The coquetry gives way, as did *The War Horses's* high rhetoric, to the specific personal illuminations of *Night Feed*[8], Eavan Boland's fourth volume:

The woman is as round
as the new ring
ambering her finger.
The mirrors wed her.
She has long since been bedded.
('Dedication')

The unequivocal note of mature knowledge sounded here pervades the entire collection, as poems relate a new kind of self-awareness. Womanhood is no longer the racked identity crisis of suburbia or the relentless paring-down of 'the self', but a realisation, as the title poem has it, of the "long fall from grace". The poems are set, typically, at dawn or late evening, with the house nestled in its own existential hinterland of garden, children asleep in their room. Here, at the turning-points of daily routine, the backgrounds of ordinary life take over and assume an almost archetypal significance:

The light goes out.
The blackbird
takes up his part.
I wake by habit.

I know it all by heart:
these candles
and the altar
and the psaltery of dawn

and in the dark
as we slept
the world
was made flesh.

Like this 'Hymn', *Night Feed* in general restores the fragmented sense of woman as life-giver, paralleling the separate sense of selfhood which *In Her Own Image* examined. The characteristic moment of 'The Muse Mother', for instance, underscores not only the "clear eyes" and "quick critical sense" which Eavan Boland's poems manifest, but also that sense of 'marginality' or isolation to which she refers in the *Studies* essay.

Watching "a mother hunkering—/her busy hand/worrying a child's face", the poet's "mind stays fixed" as the woman and boy "moves away":

she might teach me

a new language:
to be a sybil
able to sing the past
in pure syllables,

limning hymns sung
to belly wheat or a woman,
able to speak at last
my mother tongue.

It is from this point in her work that the sense of isolation becomes more acute, much more at issue. For, even while the family takes precedence in much of *Night Feed,* as the very title suggests, poems such as 'Lights' and 'After a Childhood Away from Ireland' record Boland's ambiguity about the meaning of 'home'. When she writes in the latter poem,

Love is also memory.

I only stared.
What I had lost
was not land
but the habit
of land,
whether of growing out of,
or setting back on,
or being defined by ...

the unmoored speculation casts a questioning, disturbed shadow over the world of *Night Feed*. This is echoed, perhaps too consciously, in 'The New Pastoral':

I'm in the dark.
I am a lost,
last inhabitant—
displaced person

in a pastoral chaos.

Boland's "quick critical sense" urges the poem too forcibly to its chosen theme, and several other poems in *Night Feed* are flawed by the same insistence. 'It's a Woman's World', '"Daphne with her thighs in bark"' and the poems in the final section, with the exception of 'A Ballad of Beauty and Time', are pared so finely that their design upon us becomes transparent and the guiding light of subjectivity is overshadowed by Boland's critical intelligence.

IV

The Journey and Other Poems[9] is Eavan Boland's most satisfying collection to date. It is buoyed up with great confidence and its technical range is impressive, striking a balance between *New Territory* and *The War Horse* on the one hand, and *In Her Own Image* on the other. The poems follow on from *Night Feed* by taking the images of childhood and memory into direct contact with the poet's present experience. Like *Night Feed,* there is an indefinite, persistent sense of isolation.

In 'An Irish Childhood in England: 1951', Boland's feelings of separateness and exile turn 'language' into an object of self-consciousness:

... a freckled six-year-old,
overdressed and sick on the plane
when all of England to an Irish child

was nothing more than what you'd lost and how:
was the teacher in the London convent who
when I produced 'I amn't' in the classroom
turned and said—'you're not in Ireland now'.

Several of the poems in *The Journey* go behind this recollection and contemplate the relationship between 'language' and 'memory', asking which accommodates the other: does memory produce the language that becomes the poem, or is the poem the force that reproduces the memory?

The Journey concentrates upon this enigma and what it says about our knowledge of everyday life. Consistently throughout the collection Boland questions the viability of her own experience in an effort to find an appropriate poetic for it:

In the dusk
I am still
looking for it—
the language that is

lace ...
('Lace')

She remarks in 'Mise Eire' that

a new language
is a kind of scar
and heals after a while
into a passable imitation
of what went before

while 'The Oral Tradition' relates

the oral song
avid as superstition,
layered like an amber in
the wreck of language
and the remnants of a nation.

In 'The Bottle Garden', the "gangling schoolgirl" reads the *Aeneid*: "the Styx, the damned, the pity and/the improvised poetic of imprisoned meanings". If "meanings" are "imprisoned", the "improvised poetic" is what Eavan Boland's poetry has been striving for: a way of breaking through. However, in the title poem the poet receives advice and a warning about this struggle from Sappho, the great poet of Lesbos, whom she meets in a dream encounter:

> 'what you have seen is beyond speech,
> beyond song, only not beyond love;
> ....
> 'I have brought you here so you will know forever
> the silences in which are our beginnings ...

Sappho chastises the poet—"do not define these women by their work"—and opens a mysterious pact between Boland's imagination and an imaginary world that transcends the everyday domestic one she celebrates. This imaginary world anchors the personal, impermanent and vulnerable memories with which *The Journey* starts off:

> indefinite and infinite with hope,
> is the horizon, is the past and all
> they look forward to is memory.
>
> ('Growing Up')

> Years ago I left the guest house
> in the first September light
> with no sense
> I would remember this.
>
> ('There and Back')

> It came to me one afternoon in summer ...
>
> ('The Wild Spray')

The poems of *The Journey* have displaced the intensity of *In Her Own Image* with a grander assertive range, such as one finds in the title poem, 'Listen. This is the Noise of Myth', and in the strange concluding poem, 'The Glass King', which is about the mad 14th-century French king Charles VI, who in his later years believed he was made from glass:

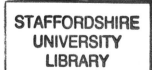

My prince, demented

in a crystal past, a lost France, I elect you emblem
and ancestor of our lyric: it fits you like a glove—
doesn't it?—the part; untouchable, outlandish,
esoteric, inarticulate and out of reach

of human love ...

It is a perplexing choice for Boland to make, since her work is so intimately bound up with "human love" and the suggestiveness of that "subtle fire" of sexuality to which Sappho herself refers in one of the surviving fragments of her poems. Similarly, while the meditations on language which characterise Eavan Boland's more recent work provide her poetry with an intellectual order, they also threaten to distract rather than strengthen the imaginative focus on her 'self'.

In contrast, however, one sees how Eavan Boland can move further through what she calls, in 'The Journey', "love's duress", as in the impeccable clarity of 'The Briar Rose':

I could be
the child I was, opening

a bedroom door
on Irish whiskey, lipstick,
an empty glass,
oyster crêpe-de-Chine

and closing it without knowing why.

The decorum is charged here with rich metaphorical possibility—of a door opening upon human activity. Yet at this stage of her writing Eavan Boland seems more committed to ideas about language than to using the language she has found, as a means of following the sure imaginative instincts which 'The Briar Rose' embodies. This is an approach that few poets in Ireland have taken seriously, but Paul Durcan may be one of the chief exceptions.

V

Since quite early in his poetic career, Durcan has seen how central to

Irish life is the relationship between family life, sexuality and authority. Hovering over this relationship in Durcan's poetry is the devilish angel of fantasy. In his writing to date, he has been unrelenting in his exposure of the kinds of hypocrisy, deceit and repression that underlie this basic relationship of power. Poetry is one way, perhaps *the* way, of redistributing justice and praise in favour of those who defy the courts of convention. In this defiance, Durcan sees women as being the strongest.

'Outside the Descent of the Holy Ghost', from his collection *O Westport in the Light of Asia Minor*, has a male figure watching a young woman weave her "sensual path into the black shadows of the porch". A family group distracts the poet momentarily before he is 'safe' from them again:

> I think of you—young woman on the church steps—
> Of how families are made—or not made—
> Of how I am my daughters' father and I pray
> May they not inherit the world of the family
> And the murderous animal of possession.
> Dear nameless woman, suntrap, scarp of snow,
> If you should see the hawthorn blossom on a day in winter
> Relish the actuality, do not flinch from pain.[10]

The plea for freedom, coupled with a recognition of its costs, is sounded throughout Durcan's work. Better, he insists, to pay that price than to submit, as so many men do in their roles as father and husband, to the mind-forged manacles of convention. In contrast, women represent and embody freedom, rebelling against the feeble conspiracies of male fantasies by living in much closer harmony with their true selves. In both theme and style, the contrast with Boland's work could not be more pointed.

It is in the search for a 'true' self that Paul Durcan's abundant imagination is brought to the boiling-point. A typical day of self-seeking is depicted in 'Phoenix Park Vespers':

> The hurriedly-emptying October evening skies neither affirmed nor
> denied
> A metaphysics of sex
> But reflected themselves merely in the fields below
> As flocks of kindred-groups, courting couples, and footballers,

Old men, and babes, and loving friends,
And youths and maidens gay,
Scattered for homes.

The "scattered for homes" reveals life as an inarticulate, closed-in existence of frustration and unhappiness, while the out-of-doors world is traversed by the freedom-loving spirit of women:

With MacDara I found myself walking
Behind a young woman in her light summer wear.
If we were walking, she was riding
The clear waters of her cotton dress
And I thought: had I the choice I had been a woman—
Instead I am strung up on a cloud called mind.
Even were I to walk naked my body were a cumbersome coat.
O fortunate soul, walking on her hips through the Green.
('On a June Afternoon in Saint Stephen's Green')

To be "fortunate", in Durcan's reading, is to be like the female figures of 'Nessa', 'Anna Swanton' or 'The Girl with the Keys to Pearse's Cottage', Cait Killann:

Often she used linger on the sill of the window;
Hands by her side and brown legs akimbo;
In sun-red skirt and moon-black blazer;
Looking toward our strange world wide-eyed.

Receptive to the world, rather than cowed by it, the woman in Durcan's poetry challenges all the mindless routine that is taken for life in "our strange world":

Outside in the rain the powers-that-be
Chemist, draper, garda, priest
Paced up and down in unspeakable rage
That we could sit all day in Teresa's Bar
'Doing Nothing'.
(Teresa's Bar)

In 'Teresa's.Bar', 'Doing Nothing', like looking 'wide-eyed', is an honourable thing, since it is part of that "process in which there is no contradiction/For those with guts not to be blackmailed by time". Time is, in Durcan's poetry, the great enemy ("Black time" as he calls it), and his images of clocks and the imposing will of duty reach a mythical culmination in the form of de Valera, the embodiment of history:

> I see him now in the heat-haze of the day
> Blindly stalking us down;
> And, levelling an ancient rifle, he says 'Stop
> Making love outside Áras an Uachtaráin.'
> ('Making Love outside Áras an Uachtaráin')

In contrast to this vision, Durcan playfully turns the clock back in 'Backside to the Wind', where the 14-year-old "rambling alone/By the scimitar shores of Killala Bay" dreams "of a French Ireland":

> Father Molloy might be a worker-priest
> Up to his knees in manure at the cattle-mart;
> And dancing and loving on the streets at evening
> Backside to the wind.

The dreaming blur fixes, though, upon reality;

> I walk on, facing the village ahead of me,
> A small concrete oasis in the wild countryside;
> Not the embodiment of the dream of a boy,
> Backside to the wind.

What follows is a litany of dispossession as the failed dream pitches into blank statement—"money is our God":

> Seagulls and crows, priests and nuns,
> Perch on the rooftops and steeples,
> And their Anglo-American mores asphyxiate me,
> Backside to the wind.

For Durcan these 'mores' are everywhere stamped upon the physical landscape: "the daylight nightmare of Dublin city", in the "glass-paned door of our grim suburban home", where

> Another dry holocaust in the urban complex over;
> Over another stagger home along the semi-detached gauntlet;
> Another day done.

The man in 'The Daughters Singing to their Father' symbolises that deadly defeat of the spirit which Durcan sets his poems to rectify:

No matter what bedlam or vacuum the night may rear
He will hear only his daughters singing to him
From behind the arabic numerals of the clock:
'There is no going back, boy, there is no going back.'
Long will he gaze into the clock, and to that last spouse
Under the skyline—for his daughters give thanks.

It is with the likes of Teresa, "bringer of dry wisdom and free laughter", or of Marguerite, "a convent girl" with "apple blossom cheeks ... bronze curls,/And ... eyes forever looking-upwards" ('Marguerite'), or a Fat Molly, with her relishing earthiness, that Durcan's imaginative vision is redeemed:

And she used make me kiss her for hours non-stop
And I'd sit in her lap with my hands
Around her waist gulping her down
And eating her green apples
That hung in brunches from her thighs
And the clusters of hot grapes between her breasts
Until from the backs of my ears down to my toes
All of me tingled ...

('Fat Molly')

Who exactly 'me' or 'I' is in the marvellous dream worlds that Durcan creates does not matter; the poet's 'self' does not enter his poems as a defining force; 'it' is rather another circumstance to which the poems refer. One accepts this condition on faith, or not, in which case the poems seem ridiculously unbelievable fabrications that "over-saturate their subjects".[11]

In Durcan's poetry, man tends to compare very badly with woman. She typically figures as enchantress, in touch with a richer, fuller life than he. Men—among them Donal Dowd in 'The Day of the Starter'; 'The Limerickman who Went to the Bad'; "the do-it-yourself-men boors/Who detest men with feminine souls,/Boors who when they were boys/Spoke of women as 'ruddy holes'" ('Polycarp'); the apologist for terrorism who

... whines into my face: 'You must take one side

or the other, or you're but a fucking romantic.'
His eyes glitter hate and vanity, porter and whiskey,
('In Memory; The Miami Showband: Massacred 1 July 1975')

and the Professors Cantwell, in 'Two History Professors Found Guilty of Murder', have merely caricatured life

... in a country where words also have died an unnatural death
or else have been used on all sides for unnatural ends
and by poets as much as by gunmen or churchmen.
('Tribute to a Reporter in Belfast, 1974')

Occasionally, women are guilty of such failings. The middle-class woman who speaks in 'Three Hundred Men Made Redundant' is absorbed in her daily round of visiting the butcher's and the hairdresser's and complaining to the priest that "the handrail has become a bit sticky". The refrain underlines the senselessness of her prattle:

But we have bigger issues to thrash out
Than 300 men made redundant;
For example the evils of family planning—
Not to mention mixed marriages and mixed education.

The victims of this world—such as Ted Rice, the tragi-comic married man who fell in love with a semi-state body (in the poem of that name) or 'The Butterfly Collector of Corofin'—are presented as no longer capable of dealing with the lies and hypocrisies. Another strategy Durcan uses is to reverse the traditional role-playing by a surrealistic shift of the familiar into the exotic: 'Margaret Thatcher Joins the IRA', 'Bishop of Cork Murders his Wife', 'The Man Whose Name Was Tom-and-Ann', 'On Seeing Two Bus Conductors Kissing', and so on. In spite of the obvious comic intention of such titles, there is an underlying serious examination of the world in which violence, sexism and political expediency are taken for granted. This is also the case when Durcan turns his attention to explicitly sexual matters. 'The County Engineer' who "is a dragon on the site" becomes something quite different in the hands of his wife, while in 'The Archbishop Dreams of the Harlot of Rathkeale' the archbishop's displaced male sexuality resorts to bizarre fantasy:

I am simply lying here in my double-bed
Dreaming of the harlot of Rathkeale;
I see her walking down the road at evening
Wearing a red scarf and black high-heel shoes;
She is wearing nothing else and the sun
In the western sky is a-dying slowly
In a blue sky half as old as time
...
She is walking towards me when the dream ends
And I wake up in the morning feeling like an old bull
Plumb to charge through my brethren in my sermon.

Throughout all this marvellous boundless energy, Durcan returns to a central image of potential transcendence: the sea, with its landscapes and estuaries. Water—associated with baptism and birth, and ultimately with the self-knowledge of womanhood—comes to symbolise tranquillity. In 'Ballina, Co. Mayo', "young men and old men/Stand on the bridge watching the waters flow under them":

They lean their elbows on the wall with their hands cupped as if in prayer;
But though they may in themselves be kneeling
They are standing squarely on the callous pavement.

The sense of supplication, so much a hidden part of Durcan's poetry, of the blessing that nature bestows ("The air is full of reasonableness") is confirmed by

And if at their life's end they whisper for a priest
It may be because of what they can hear among all these waters' silences and sounds.
Such as the tiny object that being borne along helplessly upon the waters
Is seeming to say: *Let this chalice pass from me ...*

The prayer is totally in keeping with the genuinely Catholic sensibility which Durcan's poems manifest, as in the centrality of the mother/woman figure. In 'Hymn to Nessa', she is directly linked with nature's life force:

When I looked back again she was not gone
She was sleeping under the sun
When I looked back again she was not gone
She was sleeping under the sun.

The kind of identification such a poem makes, as a song of praise, reveals the characteristic spirit of Durcan's poetry as a whole: uncomplicated, but fiercely intense. Moving from its bustling energy to Thomas McCarthy's poetry is like returning indoors from the noisy streets of a city carnival. For McCarthy's poems are pervaded by a quiet, introspective stillness and an almost autumnal air of melancholia.

VI

Thomas McCarthy's first collection, *The First Convention* (1977)[12], was praised for its mature tone of voice in a poet so young (he was then 23). The collection also signified, as Eavan Boland remarked in her review of it in *The Irish Times*[13], "that rare and long-awaited advent in Irish poetry; a glimpse of de Valera's Ireland, through the eyes of a poet born into the officially declared Irish Republic. Here is a scrutiny of the dream in the punishing light of the reality". Boland, referring to one poem in particular, 'State Funeral', spoke of its "convincing, unrhetorical statement", and this is the general impression one has of McCarthy's poetry: a clearly focused scene set forth with meticulous care, like a precious stone reset by a jeweller.

Experience has an absolute value in McCarthy's poems; it is his poetry's guiding light, as when he describes his father's 'Last Days in the Party':

> Trapped in that jungle of old
> Men, I made a beacon of your word-play.
>
> Tonight, father, master of tough language,
> It's you I find trapped on a tightening
> Syntax; pulled out of depth. The young man
> In the trendy suit laughs when he takes
> Your place. His broad smile is your dead
> Old cheer; a flourish without permanence.

If the past has a heroic dimension in McCarthy's poetry, he rarely lets it off the hook of present needs and perceptions of failure. There is a deceptive realism in McCarthy's work which can easily be misinterpreted as nostalgia. Ironically, though, his search through the past—"the force of national politics soft-/ening in the huge quietness of the dark"—reveals itself as a search for authority, a position that enables the poet to measure and judge.

One regularly comes across the figure of the father and his emblematic surrogates in writing by Irishmen. It is as if the struggle for national independence left too many men as *young* men, sapped of their emotional energy but unable to grow up. For the generations that followed, this spiritual legacy manifested itself as a kind of haunting shadow of greatness, dedication and high ideals, but also an atmosphere of stunted growth, time-locked and enervating habit and belief. This is, after all, what Stephen Dedalus registered in the passage quoted earlier on as he watched "his father and his two cronies" revel in "the memory of their past". It is present too in McCarthy's poem 'State Funeral', with its Joycean epigraph—"Parnell will never come again, he said. He's there, all that was mortal of him. Peace to his ashes"—and in the poem's concluding stanza, where the assumed immortality of greatness, de Valera, is laid to rest:

It was a landscape for old men. Today
They lowered the tallest one, tidied him
Away while his people watched quietly.
In the end he had retreated to the first dream,
Caning truth. I think of his austere grandeur;
Taut sadness, like old heroes he had imagined.

It is the "austere grandeur" which animates McCarthy's imagination, inspired by his father's example, and dramatised in the Yeatsian stance of long, well-filled stanzas, the languid gardens and domestic interiors that assume a frieze-like, abundant clarity.

In McCarthy's second collection, *The Sorrow Garden* (1981)[14], this clarity settled much too comfortably upon its subjects, and what in the earlier book had been distinctive became immobilised with coffee-table-book impressionism:

... at night, I imagine, she would lie awake
And listen to the mountains for her own sake.
She would listen to the linen wind at night
As it flapped the wet clothes. She would steal
Into the children's room to dream and write;
To be a whole person, a picker of bluebells.

('The Poet of the Mountains')

The Sorrow Garden draws too much attention to its author as a person who reads, thinks and writes about poetic moments. The second poem of the collection, for example, unhappily mixes metaphorical 'you' and 'I' with images of war—"a war I never lived/but possess deeply on occasions", recalling how "you found the first Collected Carlos/Williams" and "gave it to me, thirty years later,/as a gift of peace, the pages fading at the edge".

The sense of sanctity here, of precious gifts whose meaning challenges the world's corruptions, enfeeblements and pain, is never adequately focused in *The Sorrow Garden.* Possibly the reason for this is McCarthy's indecision about who is talking; the possession of the 'self' in the book is blurred and uncertain. We find no appropriate compensation in the domineering figures of de Valera and the Brigadier, the leading light of AE, Mac Liammóir, Parnell, Francis Stuart and Isaac Bashevis Singer, and the literariness that pervades the book. McCarthy is aware of the problem. In 'The Provincial Writer's Diary', he writes,

> Everything became consumed by the Personal:
> furious theatre work killed some time,
> strolling with his bachelor friends, fishing,
> or the steady cumulative ritual of walking
> beyond the city to sketch its grey limits.
> But nowhere could he find (within those limits
> of thought) the zeal that would consume life.

The "zeal" is what *The Sorrow Garden* palpably lacks, overshadowed, as the collection so clearly is, by the death of the poet's father. The absence seems to underline other absences as well (emotional, as much as cultural and political) and the imaginative responsiblity to replenish these is the burden which *The Sorrow Garden* buckles under. It shows the strain of a too literary self-consciousness in conflict with its own imaginative intuitions, a conflict that is only reconciled, significantly, by the father's understanding:

> My father became famous on his word-journeys,
> sailing (on extended leave) with Scott, avenging
> all crime with *Four Just Men.* Every book I open
> brings him to the window to strain his weak eyes
> and answer our long calls with a wave of his pen.

('My Father, Reading')

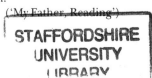

It is therefore hardly surprising that the opening poem in McCarthy's third collection, *The Non-Aligned Storyteller* (1984)[15], should be in praise of an older writer, Claud Cockburn:

> After years of bitterness, an excessive
> Dialectic of dreams and writing, is
> One sweet reward for having fought alone—
>
> Though words are never left alone.

Recurring throughout the collection is McCarthy's basic theme: the repossession of the past—his family's and his country's—and the *need* to prove the artistic and imaginative viability of this project. He runs the risk, however, of protesting too much, as in 'Counting the Dead on the Radio, 1972', while the absence of a mocking self-irony makes lines such as the following appear unbearably gauche:

> We read books as hungrily as Edmund
> Burke, with more affection than any dauphiness.

The Non-Aligned Storyteller is, in spite of its title, the most 'political' of McCarthy's collections to date, in that he is dramatising the lives of those who are themselves 'involved in politics', either directly or as writers. The shopkeepers, the ministers of state, the by-now emblematic figure of "my father", the elders, chairman, president, the "glitter" and "talk" about the past and conflicts—all dissolve in 'Question Time' to "the prize is a week in Brussels, money for two,/ and kisses from two Euro-MPs just passing through". If this is not the *punishing* light of reality which Eavan Boland saw in McCarthy's first collection, it is probably all the more real in exposing 'the dream'.

Notes

[1] James Joyce, *A Portrait of the Artist as a Young Man* (London: Jonathan Cape, 1926), p. 108.

[2] Hélène Cixous, *The Exile of James Joyce* (New York: David Lewis, 1972), p. 72.

[3] Eavan Boland, 'The Woman Poet in a National Tradition', *Studies*, Summer 1987, pp. 148-58.

[4] Cixous, *The Exile of James Joyce*, p. 92.

[5] Eavan Boland, *New Territory* (Dublin: Allen Figgis, 1967).

[6] Eavan Boland, *The War Horse* (London: Victor Gollancz, 1975).

[7] Eavan Boland, *In Her Own Image*, with drawings by Constance Short (Dublin: Arlen House, 1980).

[8] Eavan Boland, *Night Feed* (Dublin: Arlen House; London: Marion Boyars, 1982).

[9] Eavan Boland, *The Journey and Other Poems* (Dublin: Arlen House; Manchester: Carcanet, 1986).

[10] Paul Durcan, *The Selected Paul Durcan*, ed. Edna Longley (Belfast: Blackstaff Press, 1982). All subsequent quotations from Durcan's poetry are taken from this volume.

[11] Edna Longley, Introduction to *The Selected Paul Durcan*, p. xv. There, she states, "No loader of every rift with ore, though capable of startling concentration, Durcan resembles D.H. Lawrence in his tendency to write 'the poetry of the present moment', or adopt a biblical style of prophecy. But whilst some poems over-saturate their subjects—some titles nearly exhaust them!—he can also renew the simplest ballad-forms."

[12] Thomas McCarthy, *The First Convention* (Dublin: Dolmen Press, 1978).

[13] Eavan Boland, 'A New Voice in Poetry', *The Irish Times*, 22 July 1978.

[14] Thomas McCarthy, *The Sorrow Garden* (London: Anvil Press, 1981).

[15] Thomas McCarthy, *The Non-Aligned Storyteller* (London: Anvil Press, 1984).